S0-ARO-122

"I love Zach Hunter's heart, and I love *Lose Your Cool*. Couldn't put it down. Too often we either lack passion or get passionate about what doesn't matter. Zach's outstanding book is about people with passion that matters—passion for Jesus that shows itself in helping those who need it most. May God use *Lose Your Cool* to touch young and old alike and radicalize our lives. May following Jesus no longer be a buzzword, but an adventurous life of joyful dependence on the God whose heart was broken and whose hands were forever scarred by his love for us and for this desperate world."

—Randy Alcorn, author, *The Treasure Principle*, *Heaven*, and *Safely Home*

"*Lose Your Cool* was the perfect reminder for me to never settle for my comfort zone; to constantly strive to use every ounce of my being to change the world. *Lose Your Cool* not only is well-researched and well-versed, but it's also interactive so readers have the chance to discover their own unique passions, as well as the significance of being passionate about the right things."

—Alyson Stoner, actress, *Camp Rock*, *Cheaper by the Dozen*, *Step Up 3*

"I love Zach, and I love his heart. At a young age he understands that once you've tasted purpose, it's really hard to be satisfied with mere existence. He's a leader in a growing group of young people that understands our time on earth is a gift—they don't want to waste it."

—Jeff Foxworthy, comedian, author, host of *Are You Smarter Than a Fifth Grader?*

DISCOVERING A PASSION THAT CHANGES YOU AND THE WORLD

LOSE
YOUR
COOL

ZACH HUNTER

ZONDERVAN®

ZONDERVAN.com/
AUTHORTRACKER
follow your favorite authors

ZONDERVAN

Lose Your Cool: Discovering a Passion that Changes You and the World
Copyright © 2009 by Zach Hunter

Requests for information should be addressed to:
Zondervan, *Grand Rapids, Michigan 49530*

ISBN 978-0-310-28516-8

International Trade Paper Edition

All Scripture quotations, unless otherwise indicated, are taken from the *Holy Bible, New International Version*®. NIV®. Copyright © 1973, 1978, 1984 by International Bible Society. Used by permission of Zondervan. All rights reserved.

Any Internet addresses (websites, blogs, etc.) and telephone numbers printed in this book are offered as a resource. They are not intended in any way to be or imply an endorsement by Zondervan, nor does Zondervan vouch for the content of these sites and numbers for the life of this book.

All rights reserved. No part of this publication may be reproduced, stored in a retrieval system, or transmitted in any form or by any means — electronic, mechanical, photocopy, recording, or any other — except for brief quotations in printed reviews, without the prior permission of the publisher.

Interior design by Brandi Etheredge Design

Printed in the United States of America

09 10 11 12 13 14 15 • 24 23 22 21 20 19 18 17 16 15 14 13 12 11 10 9 8 7 6 5 4 3 2 1

Dedicated to Minnie Broas

Miss Minnie was many things: Faithful, loving, tough, protective, and joyful. But in all these things she was passionate. Even while battling the cancer that ended her earthly life, she trusted God to be her everything. In my mind she will always be a symbol of unbridled passion.

I dedicate this book to you, Miss Minnie. May your legacy live on and your story constantly inspire us to live like the real Jesus. We miss you.

TABLE OF CONTENTS

By Joel Houston—Hillsong United, Australia

Here's the thing: I like chicken. I especially like the grilled kind with gravy and green beans and baked potatoes—the kind you find served backstage at just about every music festival event I've ever had the chance to attend.

And so it was, at such an event in the canyons of Washington State, having worked up a solid hunger and in full-chow-mode, that I found myself abruptly disrupted from the spoils of my gravy-laden-poultry. A disruption that was by all means no small thing given all that was going on at the time, and not the least because...well...I like my chicken! And yet here I was in a festival greenroom surrounded by the who's who of Christian pseudo-celebrity-dom, the atmosphere a mix-mash of festival buzz, the distant pounding of bass and drums, and kids screaming, jumping around in imitation Ray-Bans and every kind of band-hero tee-shirt, and enjoying all that the day and the moment had to offer. All the while back-stage, real-life-band-heroes are catching up, sharing on-the-road adventure stories, talking instruments and gear, admiring each other's haircuts, skinny jeans, and slogan-adorned tee-shirts—everyone enjoying their chicken...

And yet in the midst of all the frivolous conversation my ears are tuned to a (then) 14-year-old kid speaking enthusiastically about...wait for it...the potential for young people to help abolish slavery in all its forms! I was stunned, and immediately I found myself searching for clarification. Was I hearing this correctly? Was this kid just rehashing a recently researched school assignment on William Wilberforce or was this for real? I took the super-sleuth approach to eavesdropping and motioned my attention falsely towards my dinner, though clearly my senses were firmly focused elsewhere.

Caught off-guard, I was captivated—not so much by the depth of his insight (which was deep), nor his lack of years (which were few), nor even, for all its urgency, the topic of conversation (which was astonishing). The thing that arrested my attention so completely was his passion—a certain conviction that spoke louder than all the noise in that room. I was no longer interested in who else was there, or what guitar they were now using, or what band was temporarily doing their thing on main stage, or even how much my stomach was desperately craving the chicken and gravy and beans and baked potatoes now left abandoned on the plate in front of me.

None of it seemed to matter anymore, rendered meaningless in the scheme of things by the passionate idealism of a 14-year-old kid from the U.S.

Fast-forward three years and here I am writing the foreword for this kid's third book. He's no longer a kid, but a young man, still passionate about seeing a generation use its gifts, talents, and passions to stand for peace, love, and justice. This is the challenge for our generation; to choose to live a life that goes beyond ourselves when everything is geared towards us; to listen, to speak, and to make a stand for something that counts.

But in our day and age it's hard sometimes to distinguish anything amidst all the noise; so much information fighting for our attention that we never really hear anything. So many options laid out at our disposal that we run the risk of never really doing anything. The reality is, we can do whatever we want with our time here on earth, but if we want our lives to count, we can't afford to be silent any longer, we can't conform any longer to the patterns of apathy and indifference. God's plan has always been his people. His plan is us, and that means he has chosen *you* for such a time as this. Not one day someday when you've finished college, or you have a degree, or you're a real life band hero, or once you've finished your chicken or whatever. Our time is now, and though it might seem like we don't have what it takes to make a difference, all we need is... our passion.

We can't afford to lose it, we can't waste it on ourselves, but as Zach reveals through these pages, we must use it to stand up for those who are being oppressed, and to speak out against injustice. The world we live in might be consumed in its chicken and gravy, but no matter who you are, or where you're from, or how insignificant you may feel, you have a voice, and in the midst of all the noise, it's your passion that will be heard.

This book has probably been the most difficult and emotional of the three books I've written; it would have been impossible to do this without the support of all my friends and family.

First, I would like to thank my mom for helping immensely with research and questions for the ends of chapters. I can't express enough gratitude for all she's done for me throughout my whole life. Thank you, too, Dad for helping in the editing process and for always being a supportive and trusted confidante. You both are great. To my little bro, Nate—thanks for being patient while I had to finish this book; now I'm done, and we can play Legos!

Thank you to all the families who have supported me through your prayers and otherwise, especially the Schulzes, the Parvas (much love to my "sisters"—Ellie, Ana, and Alex), the Robinsons, the Sklenars, the Foxworthys, the Moorings, and the Bennetts—love all of you lots. Thank you to Free the Slaves, IJM, Love146, Make Way Partners, and RugMark for being voices for the voiceless and bringing lasting freedom to so many. Thanks also to my friends from Hillsong who use their influence on behalf of those who have none. And thanks to all my friends from Youth Specialties and Zondervan who believed that a kid who was just 14 (then 15, then 16) could write a book (or books).

Thank you to everyone at Compassion International, especially Wess Stafford, Suzie Johnson, Rich Van Pelt, Greg Frady, and Keith Bordeaux, for continuing to teach me about a passion for the poor. Rich, I know you pray for me every day—this means more to me than you can know. Thanks to my fellow activists at Bite Back and Dry Tears: Jordan, Conner, Logan, Jared, Kyle, and Dan. And thank you to Jeremy Jones for believing that we, as a generation, have something to say.

Thank you to Alexis "MySpace" Schulze for keeping up with all of my, well, MySpace stuff. You are the best! Thanks to all of you who have gotten involved in Loose Change to Loosen Chains (LC2LC) through MySpace and Facebook. You are all abolitionists, and the world is going to be a better place because of you! Let's continue to use these tech tools to do good and not be overpowered by the evil that's there.

Thank you to all the members of the staff at Grace Fellowship Church who have invested in my life: Pastor Randy, Miss Anita, Brian and Erin, Kenny (even though you moved!), Pastor Buddy, and everyone else. My LUG group (all you luggies...too many names). My friends who've poured out their time and proved that they cared through thick and thin, especially Christian Turner, Rowan Garmon, Alyson Stoner, Ariel Schulze, Kelly Everett (you're probably really surprised!), Katie Sklenar, Will O'Kelley, Steven Greenwald, Alex and Brett Harris, Stayko Staykov, and my other friends at Heritage. Thank you to all my teachers from Heritage and PCA who prayed for me and invested in me.

A big "thank you" to Doug Davidson for being a great editor on all three of my books and for helping my voice to be understood as well as heard.

Thank you, Melody Green, for being open to a discussion about Keith. My time with you had an impact on me, and I'm really enjoying listening to my mom's old vinyls of him. He was an amazing person, and you still are!

I would also like to thank all my friends in the music industry: Jack and Leeland Mooring, The Wrecking, Lamont Hiebert, Vicky Beeching, Sara Groves, Charlie Peacock, Brooke Fraser, Joel Houston, and Jon Foreman. Your inspiration fills this book, and through you, I've made many new friends who are enriching my life. Thanks also to the authors and speakers whose work has inspired me and helped me grow, especially Randy Alcorn, Margaret Feinberg, C.S. Lewis, George MacDonald, Judah Smith, John Ortberg, and Paul Andrew. And my appreciation also goes out to my favorite poets, whose works act as muses for inspiration: Jon Foreman (yes, again), Akiane Kramarik, Amena Brown, Blair Wingo, Langston Hughes, Emily Dickinson, and King David. Thank you to Luke O'Kelley for contributing your artistic talent to this book.

I've met a lot of people from all around the world who share my passion, and I'm grateful for your partnership. I can't list you all by name, but I thank you all the same. I hope to reconnect with many of you as God allows me to travel and be inspired by all of you and how you're embracing your passion.

I also want to thank Steve Carter and the youth team at Mars Hill—thank you for believing in me from the start and, through your confidence, giving me the courage to step into what God had for me. Thank you, Justin Mayo—you are always a shot in the arm; keep doing what you are doing! Thanks to Malcolm Duplessis for his perspective on life and his wisdom about worship.

A very special thank you to the Broas family for their love and support. Daniel, you are one strong brother and a great encouragement to me.

Abba Father, Jesus, and the Holy Spirit: thank you for your love, sacrifice, and guidance that I would be incomplete without.

I'm sorry if I've forgotten anyone, but my publisher wants me to send in this manuscript RIGHT NOW!!! Love you all so much!

Peace. Love. Justice! Your brother and friend,

Zach Hunter

PASSION VS. INTEREST

HYPER-HYPERBOLE

If you spend any time at my school, you'll see that my generation says a lot of things we don't mean—or maybe it's just that we say things without considering the real meaning. We exaggerate a lot—not on purpose, but I think the way we communicate lends itself to exaggeration. We call something "awesome" when it's just "aw-right."

Because of the massive social networking sites, many of us now have a lot of "friends" whom we've never even met. There are people at school whom we might never talk with face-to-face, and might not even like, yet we call them "friends" too. Through Facebook and MySpace, the status of "friend" or even "top friend" is just a click away, instead of reserving that word for people who have shared our ups and downs and proved their loyalty over time.

Or look at tired texting terms like "LOL." I seriously doubt that most normal people laugh out loud as often as I've been led to believe. I have a friend who, in a series of just six text messages, gave me five "LOLs" and two "hahas." I'm pretty sure that if she were laughing out loud as much as she said, her parents would have sent her to therapy.

Do you get what I'm saying?

This might all seem innocent, but I think language shapes our thinking in subtle yet important ways. Words matter. When we casually and carelessly use words that were once powerful, how does this impact their meaning? More importantly, how does it impact us?

The word *love* is a great example. What does it really mean to love something or someone? In one day someone could say all these things: "I LOVE *American Idol*," "I LOVE coffee," and "I LOVE Jesus." Do those really belong in the same category? Now, I'm not saying you shouldn't love the simple things in life, and it's probably clear you don't LOVE your grandma the same way you LOVE popcorn. But I think you get my point. Our words no longer carry as much depth and meaning as they once did.

You may have heard that the ancient Greeks had five different words for love. There was a friendship love, an I-would-die-for-you-love, a romantic love, a sibling love, and a love called *agapao* that was an act of the will that put deep emotion into action. Of course I'm no expert on ancient Greek, and these are just my quick interpretations of the definitions of the five words. But I think the fact that all five of these ideas get translated as "love" really shows how diluted our language has become. It's no wonder, then, that the Internet and texting have continued to deteriorate our language, even changing the way we communicate with one another.

PLUGGED IN BUT NOT CONNECTED

Go hang out with kids, and you'll see that most of us are constantly checking the displays on our phones, logging in to our laptops, and sending texts to one person while talking with someone else. We communicate, and we're super-plugged-in, yet we're never fully connected to others or really connected to what's going on around us.

Tech devices have given us amazing access to one another. You can reach people around the world with a few keystrokes. You can track someone on a GPS and have alerts sent to your cell phone. Yet I think many teens resist having genuine, deep, and personal conversations—even with their "top friends." We text people who are across the room, and "LOL" while chatting about Algebra homework (which, if you're like me, is no laughing matter). We go to parties to get together, but many students have their ear buds in and are incessantly checking their iPhones to see if a new message has come in. With all these distractions I wonder if we may be missing God's whispers to us about our priorities and the desire he has to help us unlock some amazing ideas he wants to pursue through us.

Online, we fill out profiles that talk about the things we say are our "interests"—the things that consume our time like "playing Wii, playing baseball, my girlfriend, watching *Lost*, playing Wii, listening to music, reading my Bible, playing Wii." And chances are, if you're in some sort of dating relationship (whatever *that* means), playing Wii (or Xbox 360 or PS3) three times a day, watching TV, playing sports, and eating, you might not find the time to read your Bible—so that might need to be taken off the list of real "interests" if you're totally honest.

Maybe a level above our interests are the things we say we're "*really* passionate about." These things might include some of our interests, but they're often more specific. We may say we're really passionate about football or the Beatles. Some people say they're passionate about coffee or chocolate or their favorite TV show. I know people who will argue for hours about who should have won a reality TV show (something they feel passionate about), but won't speak up to challenge a racist comment because they don't want to offend anyone. If this sounds like you, then maybe something isn't quite right.

So what do you see when you look at the things you say you're interested in, the things you "love," and the things you're really passionate about? I think most of us would have to admit there are quite a few petty things on our personal lists. Yet these are the things that consume our time, the things we spend time thinking about and doing, the things we make a priority.

IS THIS PASSION?

Let me tell you a story about a guy named Mark Malkoff. Mark decided to try to visit all 171 Starbucks stores in Manhattan in a single 24-hour day. And he didn't just wake up one morning and decide to try this—he spent two whole months planning the effort. In those two months he bought a cheap bike from K-Mart (because, of course, he couldn't reach all 171 on foot), and he went to many of the stores to research opening and closing times and to see which ones had the longest lines at different times of day.

On the big day, he woke up at about 4:30 a.m. and started biking. He had figured out that he had to arrive at a different Starbucks every seven minutes for over 20 hours, and he wanted to order something and consume at least part of what he'd ordered in every store. At one point he had to have a friend drive him around because his body was shutting down from the overexertion and the caffeine. He even showed up at one store four minutes after closing time and had to bribe a worker $80 to let him in so he could get a piece of pound cake. He didn't arrive home until about 4 a.m. the next day.

Visiting 171 Starbucks stores in a single day is pretty crazy, no matter how much a person might LOVE coffee. But when Mark was interviewed by CNN, he confessed, "I actually don't drink coffee, which makes this thing completely insane."

When I first read Mark's story, I laughed out loud (for real—not an "LOL"). But I was really struck by the reaction of Dan Lewis, the Starbucks spokesperson of that region. When asked about Mark's stunt by the *New York Daily News*, Lewis said, "We appreciate Mr. Malkoff's passion, and we applaud his creativity and commitment."

So Mark Malkoff is now famous for being passionate, right? But what is he passionate about? Coffee? He said he doesn't even drink coffee. This is what I would call a misguided passion—or maybe it's just a desire to get his day in the spotlight. You may laugh, but what about the things we argue about all the time, the things we seem to be so passionate about: The mispronunciation of a word, whether or not a movie is good, and which band is the best, or worst. What does all that impassioned arguing get us?

I must admit, Mark Malkoff's story is amusing. But what did he really accomplish? Wouldn't it have been better if he'd gone to 171 of Manhattan's biggest charities and raised money to do some good? What if he'd taken that drive to do something his friends said is impossible—something that might even appear foolish—and decided to tackle something that would really make a difference for others? Like Malkoff, who was simply trying to make the news by doing something quirky or different, I wonder if we choose some of the things we embrace as passions just because they are odd, or because they'll get us attention, or just because.

FLAMMABLE

Now before I say any more about passion, let me clear one thing up: A lot of people hear the word *passion,* and the first thing they think of is romantic love or sexual desire. But that's not what I'm talking about here. When I refer to passion, I'm not just talking about that guy and girl at your high school who are *always* together. *Passion* can refer to anything you feel powerful emotion about.

Let's go back to the difference between an interest and a passion—because I think there *is* a big difference. An interest is often an "I want to know more" kind of thing. Many people—maybe even *most* people—claim to be interested in God or interested in helping people. This isn't a bad thing necessarily, but it is not necessarily good either. If you are one of those people, ask yourself this: "Would I give away money and time and blood to this thing I'm interested in? If I had to, would I die for this interest?" I think the answer is no. "I'm really interested in biking," you might say, but would you die to bike just one more trail?

So what is passion, really? And how is it different from interest? I'm sure others may define passion differently, but for the purpose of this book, let's be clear that passion is a good bit deeper than interest. Let's even say that, for the follower of Jesus, passion is a stirring in us that connects us more closely to the things that matter to God. That stirring moves us to a willingness to make sacrifices to accomplish something to further that passion. You can't just dig down deep inside and try to somehow draw out passion from the well of your soul. You can't go to bed tonight hoping that if you try hard enough you will be more passionate tomorrow, because passion is so much more than a simple, human feeling.

Passion often starts with an interest. Perhaps you notice some issue in your community or some problem that's facing our world, and you realize that it's wrong. Usually this awareness sparks some emotion in you, like anger or sadness—and then a realization that feeling bad simply isn't enough. You decide you want to do something about it. And that's when an interest becomes a passion. When you take the feelings inside you, or that intellectual interest you have, and put it into action, passion is ignited.

When you're passionate about something, a "whatever" attitude just won't do. You don't just sit back and stay detached. You do something. You get involved.

Sometimes passion requires going against the grain. If we're passionate about something, sometimes we'll have to give up our desire to be looked at as cool. Passion might mean sticking up for something or someone no matter what the cost. Passion, unlike interest, doesn't come from merely liking something or having fun while doing it. Passion is being willing to give up something of ourselves—our time, our resources, our comfort, our interests—for something or someone.

Some of the most passionate people since the beginning of time have been willing to give their all—even their very lives—for the causes they were passionate about. Of course not every passionate person is forced to become a martyr because of his or her passion, but every passionate person has to make sacrifices.

If you know me, you know I love a good story and that I believe we can discover things about ourselves through the stories of others. This book is filled with the stories of passionate people. Every single one of them has been willing to make sacrifices to pursue his or her particular passion. While most chapters will focus on people whose passions lead to a better world, we'll also look at the stories of a few whose passions are less admirable—or even terribly destructive. We will look at people whose passions flow directly out of their Christian faith, but we'll also seek to learn from people who aren't committed to Jesus, yet still have something to teach us. We'll unpack some pretty interesting characters on the pages that follow, and we'll ask, "What can we learn from them about passion and about ourselves?"

We'll also talk about priorities. It sometimes seems that the things we students are most passionate about are things that should be mere interests, and the things we express interest in are often things we should be truly passionate about. Sometimes we need to turn it upside down. Our generation has such amazing potential for passion, but we need to be passionate about things that matter. We'll explore that more a little later.

Do you want to be passionate? Do you want to find a reason to get out of bed in the morning? Do you wish you were so excited about a project or a purpose that you had a hard time getting to sleep at night? Do you want to "lose your cool" in a good way and discover a passion that can change you—and maybe even change the world? I know my answer to each of these questions is "yes"—and I hope yours is, too. If you'll stick with me through this book, I think you'll find these stories will ignite a flame within you.

||||| SOMETIMES THE ANSWER IS "NO" ||||||||||||

Amy Carmichael grew up in Ireland in the late 1800s. She was the oldest daughter of two devout Christians. As a little girl Amy desperately wanted blue eyes, but her eyes were brown. Her mother had taught Amy that if she prayed, God would answer. So one night, before bed, Amy prayed that God would give her eyes of "smiling Irish blue." The next morning, she hopped out of bed and ran to the mirror, but was heartbroken to see that her eyes were still brown. Her mother heard her crying, and explained that God always answers prayer, but sometimes the answer is "no." In the years that followed, Amy would learn a great deal about the power of taking even small concerns to God.

Like many children of her day, Amy went off to boarding school at a fairly young age. She had to return after only three years because her parents didn't have enough money to fund her education. When she arrived home her mother took her shopping to buy some new clothes. Although Amy found a dress she loved—it was a deep royal blue—she decided against buying it. Amy explained to her mom that Christ had begun to put her life into perspective during her time at boarding school and having new clothes mattered less to her. She said she could wait until the next year—when her parents would be in a better place financially—to buy the dress.

Amy's father died the next year when Amy was just 18, and she never bought that dress. But she had more important things on her mind—like people in her neighborhood who didn't have adequate clothing.

THE SHAWLIES

In Ireland at the time, the girls who worked in local factories were known as "shawlies," because they didn't have enough money to buy hats to wear to church, so they covered their heads with shawls instead. Not having a proper hat was considered a disgrace. The shawls were an obvious reminder of the girls' poverty and social status, and no "respectable" person wanted anything to do with the shawlies.

Although she was just 18, Amy was disturbed by this prejudice and started a ministry to reach out to and educate these girls. Her ministry grew, and at one time, more than 300 people were being served by Amy's outreach.

> "You can give without loving. But you cannot love without giving."
> —Amy Carmichael

Amy struggled with a sickness called neuralgia—a disease of the nervous system that resulted in moments of sharp, stabbing pain. Her illness made it hard for her to work, and her family continued to struggle financially and was forced to move to try to find a better situation. Even though her own family was having difficulty, Amy felt as though God was telling her she should go out into the world and help the poor. Her heart was heavily burdened for those who suffered under the weight of extreme poverty. She spoke of dreams where she heard God's voice—as loud and clear as if he were standing right beside her—telling her to "Go." Her response was a lot like the first response Moses gave when God told him to go: "Surely, Lord, you don't mean it," she said. But over time she became certain God was calling her to go out into the world and share his love with those who were suffering.

Because of her neuralgia and her young age, Amy found it difficult to find anyone willing to take her out of the country to work among the poor. Nearly everyone she asked said no. Finally, she joined a group of women who were going to Japan as missionaries. Amy went with them and served God in Japan for as long as she could. But the work took a toll on her, and her neuralgia soon forced her to leave. However, someone told her the air in India might be better for her health, so off she went.

> "This foolish plan of God is wiser than the wisest of human plans, and God's weakness is stronger than the greatest of human strength."
> —1 Corinthians 1:25 (NLT)

A CHANCE TO DIE

In Bangalore, India, Amy learned that many girls were sold or given up by their families to serve as forced prostitutes in the Hindu temples. (I know this sounds really strange, but it was a common occurrence.) She met a little girl named Preena (which means pearl-eyes), who had run away from the temple. The plight of young girls like Preena tore at Amy's heart. She knew she had to do something about it.

In India it was hard for a white person like Amy to spend time among the poor without drawing attention to herself. So Amy came up with a disguise that helped her avoid being detected. She wore a sari, the traditional dress of women in India, and used tea bags to dye her skin dark brown. Amy realized then that God's response to her prayer request years earlier—the "no" that came when she asked for blue eyes—was actually an answer that would enable her to help many. Amy's brown eyes made her disguise more convincing. If she'd had blue eyes, she'd have never been able to mix with the crowd in a land where everyone was brown-eyed. She began to understand that her brown eyes were a gift from God.

Here's how I imagine what a day in India might have looked like for Amy:

She is just one of many women walking into the temple that day. Although she smells rather strongly of tea, she looks just like all the other women. She ascends the temple steps and pauses to look around, her heart pounding so loud she can hear it. Her breathing quickens. She moves slowly to avoid bringing attention to herself. As she glances around the nearly silent room, she makes eye contact with one young girl being held as a slave in the temple. She shuffles over and stands directly in front of the girl, slowly reaches behind her back, and offers her hand to the girl. There is no response at first, and she fears the girl will not accept her offer of help. Amy tries to control her breathing, on the edge of panic. Finally, she feels a small hand slide into her own. She grasps the hand firmly and holds it for a split second, glancing up to see if she's been noticed. Then the two girls begin walking quickly toward the door.

"Hey, what are you doing?" a voice cries out, and Amy breaks into a sprint, never letting go of the precious little hand. More angry voices in the temple as the chase begins. Slap, slap, slap—the sound of running feet echoes across the floor like small explosions. Down the steps, into the street, running for freedom—for life. Turning right, away from the temple, practically dragging the little girl behind her. "Stop! Stop!" come the angry shouts from behind again. The temple officials are in hot pursuit. Making a left turn, a right, then another left. Finally, a dead end! But Amy and the girl are gone...

Amy rescued and cared for hundreds of girls—and later boys, too—over the course of her lifetime. Every single one of those young people called her *Amma*, which means mother. They were all her children, and she took care of them with a mother's tender care.

Amy once received a letter from a girl who was considering going into missionary work. The girl asked what missionary life was like, and Amy responded by saying this: "Missionary life is simply a chance to die." After giving her own life for others over many years, when Amy passed away, her children buried her in the garden near where she lived. Since Amy had made it clear that she wanted no gravestone, they placed a birdbath over her grave with a single-word inscribed on it—Amma.

STRENGTH IN WEAKNESS

It's really interesting how some things we may not like about ourselves, or things we view as weaknesses, can be used by God to accomplish his purposes. Those characteristics that we may think are unattractive, or that make us different from others, might actually be part of God's unique plan for us. Think about it: Amy's brown eyes that made her feel different than her family were one reason she was able to be effective in rescuing little girls from slavery. God didn't see her eye color as a weakness—it was a strength. Even Amy's youth and illness helped create opportunities for God to show his plan.

I know a lot of guys and girls who think something about the way they look is unattractive or they perceive it as a weakness. I'm

To get involved in the fight to end modern-day slavery and human trafficking, join the Loose Change to Loosen Chains campaign. www.loosechangetoloosenchains.org

sure a lot of adults think that way, too. But God doesn't view us that way. We were *created* by him, in his image. God had a purpose in making us all just the way we are.

My mom likes to talk about how, in Genesis, it says God *planted* the garden. It sounds like God didn't just speak the garden into existence with a single word. Imagine that: God choosing which plants to put here, which flowers to put there. God considered which shrub would look good next to which tree. God created the garden for his pleasure and our enjoyment. And God created each of us with the same care.

Know this, girls: God thinks you are absolutely beautiful, and all of Scripture echoes with how much he adores you. He doesn't measure you according to the world's standards or compare you with some model on a magazine cover. You are undeniably beautiful to him. You are his creation.

Guys, God thinks you are awesome. It doesn't matter if you're shorter than everyone else, less of an athlete, less muscular than other guys. God loves you just as you are. He made you, and he wants to walk closely with you like a brother.

Whoever you are, you can be certain of this: God created you, God loves you, and God can use all that you are—even the things you might think are weaknesses—for his glory and for the good of others.

Bonus Material

Visit www.loseyourcoolbook.com and read about Asha, who when she was just 12 years old asked God to send her where others were afraid to go. Find out how Asha, like Amy Carmichael, is giving her life to save others.

REDEEMING WEAKNESS

While researching this book, I have discovered many amazing people like Amy who developed a passion that came directly out of their weaknesses or perceived deficits. There are many people who find their true passion in the midst of suffering and despair. Often it is the disappointments in life that build character and prepare us to serve and to pour out ourselves for others. I know for certain that when a passion flows out of weakness and suffering, the work of God is difficult to deny. When success is pulled from the ashes, we can't take the credit—that's something only God can do.

Amy Carmichael and two children

Like anyone else, I have many faults and weaknesses. I've often talked about my own struggles with anxiety, in particular. But I have learned that God takes all that I am and redeems it for his use. I am proof that God can use anyone. I hope that's encouraging to you.

Amy's story is inspiring to me—and not just because she focused on ending slavery, which is a passion of mine. But I find it so encouraging to see how God used her—a young girl, with physical weaknesses caused by illness—to rescue slaves on another continent. He could have chosen a strong Indian man of influence who could have used his power to free people; but instead, he chose the weak to confound the strong. I like this. It gives me courage and confidence.

LOSE YOUR COOL, DISCOVER YOUR PASSION

When we talk about people who are passionate, we often think first of people pursuing things they are really good at, people working in areas where they clearly have particular strengths or gifts. How does Amy's story differ from that idea?

Read these verses: 1 Corinthians 1:25, 1 Corinthians 15:43, and 2 Corinthians 12:9. How do these verses describe weakness as a positive thing?

Is there someone in your life who has experienced suffering or who lives with something others might view as a weakness? Do you think God might want to use this challenge for his glory and the good of others? How might you encourage that person?

How about you? Is there something in your life you feel is a weakness? If so, ask God how he might use this to show his strength. Ask him to show you a plan to use your weakness to bring about good for others. Really, take a minute right now and talk to God and listen to him.

If you have a hard time viewing yourself as an amazing creation of God—if you can only see your weaknesses and inadequacies—talk to someone you trust, someone you think knows God well. Share your struggle with that person and ask for help. And pray that God would help you see yourself as he sees you.

|||||| SLAVERY LIVES ON ||||||||||||

Unfortunately the plight of child slaves didn't end with Amy Carmichael's work. Today more than 27 million people are in slavery, and it's estimated that half of them are children. I can't imagine anything more detestable than the sexual exploitation of children as slaves. But the trade flourished during Amy's day, and it continues today. When Amy wrote *Things As They Are*, a book that told the story of the caste system in India and the selling of children as temple slaves, publishers were reluctant to put out the book. They were concerned the Christian public wouldn't want to hear about such suffering, believing Christians only wanted stories of success and good news.

Many think the same thing today. My dad, Gregg Hunter, cowrote a book called *Terrify No More* about the rescue of little girls from brothels in Cambodia. People sometimes said, "I just couldn't read it—it hurt too much," or "I don't want to know about those things." I've even heard people in the Christian community say they don't want their kids to know about modern-day slavery, human trafficking, and other forms of exploitation. The church communities that feel this way might have great programs to keep their youth groups entertained, but I wonder if they're not missing out on something more—the more that comes by joining God in the battle for freedom on behalf of the poor and oppressed.

GEORGE

||||| **A FASCINATING MAN** ||||||||||||

If you ask a group of people to describe someone who's passionate, you'll probably hear a wide range of answers. Some might picture a brilliant artist, a person who stays up late at night and works on into the next morning creating a beautiful masterpiece. Others might imagine someone who gets his hands dirty—like a farmer who tills the soil and cares for the plants until harvest time. Still others may picture a pulpit-pounding preacher, someone who loves people and desperately wants them to know Jesus.

Each of these descriptions applies to George Whitefield to some extent—but he's best known for his preaching. When I first learned a bit about him, I dug around and discovered he'd preached more than 18,000 sermons in his life—although fewer than 90 of them have survived. Of those, I was able to find 59 of his sermons online. As I researched his life for this book, I often found myself getting caught up in his sermons, wanting to read them all instead of doing my research. My deadline kept me focused on the task at hand—but as soon as I'm done, I'm going to download the rest of his sermons and read them all.

George Whitefield is an amazing storyteller. But what I really love about his passionate sermons is how painfully practical they are—and how relevant for today, even though he lived more than two hundred years ago! I'm excited to introduce you to his story if you've never learned about him before.

APPRENTICE OF GOD

> "Other men seemed to be only half-alive; but Whitefield was all life, fire, wing, force."
> —Charles Spurgeon

George Whitefield was born in Gloucester, England, to Thomas and Elizabeth Whitefield. George's father died when he was only two, and his mother struggled to provide for the family. As a young boy he loved the theater, and would sometimes skip school to practice for plays. His theater background would help him later when he began speaking in public. At the age of fifteen, convinced he wasn't getting much out of school, George got his mother's permission to leave school and take a job working at an inn. He'd work all day, then stay up late studying the Scriptures, as an apprentice of God.

George's attitude changed when a student from Oxford University came to visit him and his mother. George decided he wanted to attend Oxford, so he went back to secondary school, graduated, and headed off to the university. Because his family was fairly poor, he attended Oxford as a "servitor," which meant he worked as a servant for other students to pay his way through school.

While at Oxford George hooked up with a group who called themselves the "Holy Club." I can imagine the looks I'd get if I started a club by that name today! Who would have the courage to sign up? Who would be whispered about because they thought they were qualified to join? Who'd want to pass up a couple of hours online surfing, give up watching a favorite TV show, or skip soccer practice to join the Holy Club?

This club got together every evening and focused on practices like intense Bible study, fasting, prayer, and communion. Another club requirement was that members had to visit inmates in the Oxford prison twice a week. Seems like they might have recruitment problems today. "Hey, you wanna join my club? You get to fast, pray, and read your Bible. Oh! And we go to prison twice a week." I can imagine the responses you'd get. "Uh...thanks, but...fasting? I'm kind of on a strict no-dieting diet, and, uhh, reading? Does that involve sitting still? I'm also allergic to being in enclosed spaces with criminals. Maybe next week."

The Holy Club might be a tough sell today, but the original Holy Club attracted two famous brothers: John Wesley, the founder of the Methodist denomination, and Charles Wesley, the hymn writer (author of "Hark, the Herald Angels Sing," among others). One night the Wesleys and other members of the club looked out the window to see George Whitefield on his face in the dirt praying. It began to rain, and Whitefield stayed, kneeling in the mud. That's dedication. I would love to know what he was praying about. What would make him be so dedicated that he would lie on his face in the mud?

> His emotional talks, which probably seemed strange to some, were evidence of a passion pent up in his heart and fighting to come out. George Whitefield truly lived for seeing people come to a real understanding of who God is and helping them pursue him with everything they were.

AN OUTSTANDING NOMAD

While at Oxford George suddenly became extremely ill and had to return home for nine months to recover. After George finally returned to Oxford and completed school, he was ordained by the bishop in his district. The bishop placed his hands on George's head and prayed for him, an experience George later referenced saying, "My heart was melted down, and I offered my whole spirit, soul, and body to the service of God's sanctuary."

George started preaching all around England, and his popularity grew quickly. Thousands of people from all walks of life came to hear Whitefield's impassioned speeches. David Garrick, who was then England's most famous actor, said, "I would give a hundred guineas, if I could say 'Oh' like Mr. Whitefield."[1]

> "I'd rather wear out than rust out."
> —George Whitefield

George was no ordinary preacher. He would shout, cry, and even dance if that's what it took to get his point across. At one point while preaching about heaven, he suddenly stopped in the middle of talking, looked around, and then shouted, "Hark! Methinks I hear [the saints] chanting their everlasting hallelujahs, and spending an eternal day in echoing forth triumphant songs of joy. And do you not long, my brethren, to join this heavenly choir?"[2]

After traveling all over England, he went to preach in America— "The New World." There was no Internet, no direct mail campaigns, no cell phones or texting to spread the word, yet huge crowds gathered to hear this man who was becoming a bit of a legend. He often had to teach outside in open fields and town squares because the church buildings couldn't contain all the people who wanted to come and hear. At some gatherings the number of people in attendance exceeded the number of people who lived in the town. The crowds would elbow and push and shove to come hear the "divine things" coming from the mouth of this poor boy from Gloucester, England.

Whitefield went back and forth across the Atlantic many times, increasing in popularity each time. People who'd been critical of Whitefield at first (they thought he was too enthusiastic) slowly warmed to him. He was a household name in America and was known as the "Grand Itinerant"—in the modern day, he might be called something like the "Outstanding Nomad." This makes sense since he went from town to town preaching an average of ten sermons a week—that's more than one a day! He was basically the closest thing the world had to a rock star back then.

Sometimes, during his sermons, people would drop down to the ground, as though they were dead, out of conviction. One eyewitness account from a meeting that Whitefield held said, "... by God's blessing my old foundation was broken up, and I saw that my righteousness would not save me."[3] Whitefield caused the people around him to think—and to change.

LIFE, FIRE, WING, AND FORCE

Charles Spurgeon, another famous preacher who lived about a century later, once wrote this about George Whitefield: "Often as I have read his life, I am conscious of distinct quickening whenever I turn to it. He lived. Other men seemed to be only half-alive; but Whitefield was all life, fire, wing, force. My own model, if I may have such a thing in due subordination to my Lord, is George Whitefield; but with unequal footsteps must I follow in his glorious track."[4]

If you'd like to read Whitefield's sermons, you can find them at www.anglicanlibrary.org/whitefield/sermons/index.htm

The life, fire, wing, and force described in Spurgeon's quote is exactly the type of passion I'm talking about. This passion is a fire in your bones that keeps burning, a quickening of your pulse when you hear or see someone or something, a force that cannot be contained. This is what Whitefield possessed. His emotional talks, which probably seemed strange to some, were evidence of a passion pent up in his heart and fighting to come out. George Whitefield truly lived for seeing people come to a real understanding of who God is and helping them pursue him with everything they were.

How can we get a passion like Whitefield had? At least to me that type of passion is attractive—and I think at the core of every Christian is a deep desire to have that kind of impassioned life with God. We long for a life where our walk with God is real and tangible, where Scripture comes alive in such a way that we cannot contain it. I believe that type of passion comes straight from God and is discovered when we pursue God like this:

> As the deer pants for water,
> So my soul pants for you, O God.
> My soul thirsts for God, for the living God.
> When can I go and meet with God?
> (Psalm 42:1-2)

MEMBERS OF THE HOLY CLUB

I believe that any passion that comes from God is a passion that results in things that are good, true, and beautiful—maybe not by the world's standards, but by God's standards. That is the kind of passion Whitefield had.

While we may not all develop a passion that leads us to preach sermons all over the world, I think every follower of Christ should emulate Whitefield's thirst for knowing and sharing the Word. That might look different for every person. This type of passion develops when we seek God and fall more deeply in love with him. When you get closer to God, you start to catch his love for people. And when you love people, you want to do things to help them. You want other people to personally know and embrace the truth of God's massive love for them.

So how do you get closer to God? By doing the kinds of things Whitefield did. Let's look again at what the Holy Club practiced and consider how we might implement these in our lives.

1. We can read the letters God left for us (intense Bible study).

2. We can set aside insignificant things, so we can concentrate on what matters and spend time with God—even if just for a time (fasting).

3. We can talk to God and take time to be quiet and listen to him (prayer).

4. We can do acts of service in the spirit of Jesus (like visiting those who are in prison).

I recognize that the sermon Whitefield once gave on "the heinous sin of profane cursing and swearing" definitely won't be a top download on iTunes any time soon. But I love his belief that a passion for following Jesus should result in living a life that's examined—a life where we allow God to challenge our behavior and thinking at every level. I know this isn't always popular to talk about today—and some people think it's judgmental or irrelevant to ask our fellow Christians about the language we use, the TV shows and movies we watch, and how we spend our money. But I think it's worthwhile to examine the corners of our lives and ask God to help us open them to him and in the light and goodness of his Spirit.

George Whitefield

I also think the evidence of a life examined and a life that is passionate about God is a life that's also passionate about people. That is what it really means to be like Jesus—to love people as God has loved us. And if we catch this passion early on and keep growing in our understanding of God's love for us, our passion for sharing God's love with the world will just keep growing.

LOSE YOUR COOL, DISCOVER YOUR PASSION

Is there some problem in your life that burdens you so much that you would stay in the rain, praying in the mud, waiting for an answer? What would it take to make you do something like that?

Think about the Holy Club. Are there people in your life whom you could see making this kind of commitment with you?

How might you adapt the Holy Club's tenets, or creed, to a small group of friends today? Share this concept with some friends this week and see what they think.

What is an examined life? Why is it important?

Read Psalm 139:23-24 and make these words your prayer. Take a moment with God and ask him to reveal things you need to know about yourself. This might be a good thing to do each morning or night, taking time to listen to his promptings in response.

||||| **REBEL!** |||||||||||||

Some friends of mine have started their own modern Holy Club. The tenets are a little different from the club at Oxford, but the basic idea is the same—to grow into the image of Christ. Alex and Brett Harris are twins who founded The Rebelution—a rebellion against low expectations. They argue that our culture expects too little from its young people and that students are capable of investing their lives into worthwhile endeavors. The mantra of The Rebelution is "Do hard things!" In other words, don't take the easy way out, but look for a challenge, strive for excellence, and build your character! You get the idea. You can check them out at www.therebelution.com.

QUIXOTE

||||| **RIGHT THE WRONGS** |||||||||||||

I promised that we'd go looking in some unusual places to find passionate people. And I bet that some of you have never even considered going to a musical. And maybe you only read classic literature when it's required (and even then, you'd rather read the *CliffsNotes* version). But you might be amazed by the characters you'll find onstage in a show like *Les Miserables* or in a book like *Beowulf.*

Maybe you've heard of *Man of La Mancha*—a musical inspired by Miguel de Cervantes's classic book *Don Quixote*. The musical's title character is an old man who spends day and night reading books in his library. He is tormented by the inhumanity people constantly show one another. Finally he decides he cannot tolerate the injustice any longer.

The old man puts on armor and magically becomes Don Quixote, a knight whose quest is to right the wrongs of the world. Quixote has a traveling companion, Sancho Panza, who serves as his noble squire. As the two characters mount their horses near the beginning of the musical, Quixote sings a warning to all evildoers in the world, and Sancho sings of his loyalty to Quixote.

In search of a foe to conquer, Quixote sees a would-be adversary off in the distance and exclaims, "Look, it's a giant, with four swirling arms on his back!" But Sancho replies, "What are you talking about? That's a windmill!"

Quixote charges and is thrown off his horse by the powerful arms of the "giant." Yet he remains undaunted: "My enemy, The Enchanter, must have turned the giant into a windmill at the last second!" (Maybe you've heard the term "tilting at windmills" as a description of charging to battle against an imagined foe. Well, that phrase was born out of the Quixote tale.)

SEEING THINGS DIFFERENTLY

Quixote and Sancho come upon a "castle"—really an inn. Inside, a team of muleteers (mule-drivers) have been sitting at a table, taunting and flirting with a prostitute named Aldonza. For a time she fends them off, but eventually Aldonza accepts money from a man named Pedro in advance. Right after the transaction, Sancho announces the entry of "Don Quixote, Lord of La Mancha."

Quixote walks in and is immediately captivated by Aldonza. He calls her "sweet lady" and "fair virgin." Then he sings the tender ballad "Dulcinea," which, loosely translated, means "Sweet One." Quixote sees in this woman what no one else can see and sings of her purity and beauty. While everyone else sees her as Aldonza the prostitute, to him, she is Dulcinea. His high opinion of her seems almost absurd after watching her interactions with the other men in the bar. In fact Aldonza becomes angry with Quixote, because his perception of her causes her to face who she really is.

Later, when Aldonza is alone, she asks many questions about Quixote: How can he be so honorable? Why does he try to knock down walls that are unbreakable? How can he see her as being pure? Why does he "give when it's natural to take"? In short she cannot understand why he would be so loving to someone as unlovable as she.

THE IMPOSSIBLE DREAM

Later that night Quixote is confronted by Aldonza—his lovely Dulcinea. She is still perplexed and angry, demanding that he explain why he does the crazy things he does. He tries to explain, but his answer brings her little peace. In response to his declaration that his quest is to bring some "measure of grace into the world," she spits and says, "That's for your quest!" But then she turns around awkwardly and asks softly, "What does that mean...*quest*?" And Quixote launches into one of the musical's most famous songs, "The Impossible Dream," in which he describes his quest, his mission in life:

> Quixote's quest was to bring some "measure of grace into the world."

This is my quest to follow that star,
No matter how hopeless, no matter how far,
To fight for the right
Without question or pause,
To be willing to march into hell
For a heavenly cause,
And the world will be better for this,
That one man, scorned and covered with scars,
Still strove, with his last ounce of courage,
To reach the unreachable star!

Finishing his impassioned anthem, Quixote sees one of the mule-drivers slap Aldonza for not keeping their appointment. Full of fury Quixote attacks him, knocking him unconscious. The man's friends and Sancho hear the fight and join in. Aldonza, Quixote, and Sancho knock out all the muleteers. (For those of you who think musical theater is boring—this scene answers that criticism.) The innkeeper is awakened by the racket and tells Quixote he must leave—but not before he dubs him "The Knight of the Woeful Countenance."

But then Quixote—in a signature move—says he must minister to the wounds of the muleteers. Aldonza, whom he still calls Dulcinea, thinks this is a stupid idea, but he insists that it is his duty to serve his enemies. Aldonza then says that Quixote and Sancho can go, and she'll minister to the muleteers' wounds—they're her enemies, too. But after Quixote heads upstairs to prepare to leave, the muleteers wake up, kidnap Aldonza, and rape her. Up in his room Quixote has no idea of what has happened..

> Sometimes when you pursue something passionately, you may look foolish.

KNIGHT OF THE MIRRORS

The next day Quixote finds Dulcinea and sees that she is bruised. She sings the song "Aldonza," revealing how she views herself. At the end of this very painful song, Quixote declares, "Now and forever thou art my lady, Dulcinea!" She cries out and falls to the ground.

Just then a knight shows up claiming to be the Knight of the Mirrors. He insults Dulcinea and is immediately challenged to fight by Quixote. The two attendants who accompanied the knight stand on either side of Quixote with large shields that work as mirrors. In the mirrors' reflection Quixote is forced to see himself as he appears to the world—as a fool and a madman—and he is reduced to weeping.

Later we see Quixote in his bedroom at home, lying in a coma. Quixote wakes up and reveals that he is no longer "insane"—he only remembers his conquest as a distant dream. But then Aldonza forces her way into the room; she can't bear being anyone but Dulcinea. She reminds him of his quest, his impossible dream, and he exclaims that he must leave because there are more battles to be fought. Sancho and Aldonza help him out of bed, and he begins singing the musical's first song, "Man of La Mancha." Yet his breathing becomes labored and, in mid-song, he collapses, dead.

The air suddenly becomes thick with silence. Finally Sancho says to Aldonza that it's time to go, because Quixote is dead. Aldonza says that Don Quixote will live forever. When Sancho again calls her by the name Aldonza, she rebukes him, insisting that her name is not Aldonza. She is Dulcinea.

Don Quixote pursued Dulcinea passionately. At first, he looks foolish for calling her "fair virgin" when she is a prostitute. But as the story progresses, and you see that he continues to view her as blameless and beautiful, it ceases to look foolish. And eventually, it even changes the way Aldonza views herself.

The story of Don Quixote shows how sometimes when you pursue something passionately, you may look foolish—especially if everyone else is completely unimpassioned. Quixote looked at a prostitute—someone others saw as scum or filth—and he saw a woman who was pure, beautiful, and worth fighting for. While the world saw only what she was on the outside, he made a conscious effort to look for the true person on the inside.

There are many people in our social circles—in our schools, churches, and teams—who might be viewed by some people as being unworthy of our attention. But think about the types of people Jesus hung out with—outcasts and marginalized people whom others rejected and excluded. I think he wants us to have that same kind of passion for people. Quixote knew there was more to Aldonza than the world saw. And I believe that inside of every Aldonza, there is a Dulcinea. God is in the business of making us new. He sees us as who he created us to be.

Aldonza reminds me of many wounded people I have come in contact with. Often people who are in pain will push you away if you try to reach out to them. But why is that? Why is it that hurting people try to push away those who try to get close to them? Maybe they are afraid of being hurt further by the closeness of true caring, or maybe they're just afraid of being found out and humiliated. But someone who is passionate about people, someone who loves like Jesus does, doesn't stop loving just because the people they care for respond with anger or resistance.

Don Quixote can teach us to be sensitive to the hurting of others, to be fearless in the presence of enemies, and, above all, to be honorable. Inside every one of us, I believe there's a desire to win a great victory or vanquish a great enemy. Sometimes we may end up choosing the wrong battles, be they fights with windmills or with each other. Sometimes we can get so caught up in our great battle that we accidentally step on the people who have carried us on their shoulders.

LOSE YOUR COOL, DISCOVER YOUR PASSION

Have you ever noticed people who just love a good fight? Some people seem like they don't really care what the issue is, they just like to argue. How is this different from passion? What do you think drives this?

Is there a situation where you have misinterpreted the core problem you were facing? Like Quixote battling the windmill, have you ever fought the wrong "foe"? Explain.

Who is our real enemy? How does this enemy impact our discovery of passion that is from God?

Do you think Jesus and Quixote are alike? How are they similar? How are they different?

Read 1 Corinthians 2:14. How does this explain some of the criticism or mocking people may get when pursuing God or making decisions that are not popular or cool?

Are there areas of your life where you've not been behaving the way you need to because you don't want to appear foolish? Maybe there are people you haven't been treating well, or bad habits you've developed, or you've been unwilling to speak up about your faith. Describe how you may want to change.

How do you think obedience to God might lead to uncovering your passion?

|||| **THE KNIGHT'S CODE** |||||||||||||

I've bumped into the Knight's Code of Chivalry in a few places lately—in my assignments at school and also in researching this book. Many people think the ideals of chivalry are outdated and passé. But many of these principles are not just good but straight-up biblical. What if we all (guys and girls both) viewed ourselves as peace-driven knights who lived as though our lives were a quest? Find a friend and discuss how this condensed and edited version of the Code of Chivalry can be applied in your life.

1. I will not fear evil.
2. I will never lie and will always keep my promises.
3. I will never attack from behind (modern-day verbal back-stabbing).
4. I will only fight for the sake of those who are unable to defend themselves or in the defense of justice.
5. I will exhibit self-control.
6. I will respect those authorities placed over me.
7. I will respect life and freedom.
8. I will always follow the law unless it goes against what is moral and good.
9. I will die with honor.
10. I will never abandon my quest.[1]

B.B.

||||| **RIVER OF FIRE** |||||||||||||

Passion can drive people to do crazy things. This book introduces you to people willing to risk everything for their passions. Some of those passions are noble; others are foolish or even evil. The news is filled with people whose passions lead them to put themselves in harm's way—like the mom who runs into a burning building to save her child. But what if you came home and your own house was on fire? Who or what would be worth risking your life to save?

Several years ago in a small nightclub in Twister, Arkansas, a blues band was playing, immersed in the music they loved. Both the band and the crowd were wrapped up in the emotion of the music and lyrics, letting the music transport them to another place. In the middle of the room was a large metal pail full of kerosene that had been lit on fire to heat the room. For reasons unknown two men began fighting, swinging at each other and landing punches like crazy. One man pushed the other down, knocking over the pail of fire. Everyone rushed out of the building as fire began to engulf the place.

The guitarist who'd been on stage that night said "it looked like a river of fire." He'd fled immediately when the fire started, then realized he'd left his guitar inside—so he ran back into the flames, risking his life to save that guitar. "The building was...burning rapidly," he later recalled, "so it started to fall in around me and I almost lost my life."

Foolish? Probably. What kind of man loves his music so much that he'd risk everything to save his guitar? Well, in this case, it was the legendary king of the blues, B.B. King, and his guitar was the love of his life.

BELIEVING THE LIE

Riley B. King grew up in the southern United States during the time of segregation. During his youth there were separate bathrooms and drinking fountains for white people and black people. He remembers that it didn't bother him as a kid that he couldn't drink from the same fountain as whites—segregation was all he knew. He'd been taught it was normal. Because of the brainwashing that happens when immersed in a segregated culture, he almost began to believe the lie that he was inferior.

Growing up Riley never did as well in school as he would have liked, but he had a lot on his mind. When he was just five years old, his parents divorced, and just a few years later, his mom died. He even had to live on his own for some time when he was just nine years old.

But Riley had a teacher named Luther H. Henson, who was a role model for him. His teacher spoke words of encouragement, telling young Riley that one day he'd no longer be judged based on his outward

> Sometimes the pursuit of your passion and the execution of it with excellence will buy you a seat at a table where you normally wouldn't have been invited. And sometimes, people will listen to what you have to say, just because of your reputation as a passionate person.

appearance, but just by who he was as a person. Mr. Henson set a high standard, and his words would stay with King into adulthood. Henson used to say, "You have one body. Your body is your house. If you take care of your house you can live in it for a long time, but if you don't take care of it..." meaning if you smoke, drink, etc., "... you're going to hurt your house and your house won't be able to last too long." King remembers, "I started to smoke when I was 13 and after a while, I stopped. I started to drink, and after a while, I stopped. Today, I can still hear him."

Riley learned a little bit about playing the guitar from the preacher at his local church and developed his skills further using books that he ordered through the mail. He needed to find a way to make a living, so he worked on his aunt and uncle's farm picking cotton alongside his cousin. The two boys were more productive in the fields than the other workers, so his aunt and uncle sometimes let them sleep in after late nights being out playing music.

PLAYING THE BLUES

King perfected his talents as a guitarist by going out and playing on the street corners, strategically choosing a spot where the most people walked by. He'd set up with his hat on the ground, asking for money. He recalls that when he played gospel music, people would pat him on the back and say, "Boy, that was nice. Keep it up. You're going to be good one day." But when he played the blues, people would drop money in his hat. That was when he knew he wanted to make a living as a blues singer.

In 1947 King hitchhiked to Memphis, Tennessee. At that time Memphis was a musical hub much like Nashville is today—kind of like the Hollywood of music. While there he started his own radio show called "King's Spot." He needed a catchy name, so he began calling himself "Beale Street Blues Boy," which got shortened to "Blues Boy," and eventually just "B.B."

B.B. played lots of clubs and bars, including some pretty gritty venues—such as the one where he had to run through the flames to save his guitar. The day after that fire, B.B. found out that the men who knocked over the bucket of burning kerosene had been fighting over a woman named Lucille. He named his guitar "Lucille" to remind him never to do anything foolish like fighting over a woman. Since then B.B.'s guitars have always been named "Lucille"—but the original Lucille was the guitar he saved from the fire.

Success didn't come easily to B.B. King. With his background—a motherless child living in a segregated and bigoted community and lacking a solid education—he had a lot of obstacles to overcome. He experienced many setbacks, including one that he'd relive in his memory forever. In 1955 King and his band bought a bus and named it Big Red. One day Big Red was involved in a head-on collision with a flammable gas truck. King wasn't in the bus at the time, and no one from the band was badly hurt—but one other person in the wreck was killed, and another badly burned. He later found out that his insurance had been terminated on the day of the wreck—that exact day. A woman involved in the accident sued King for a million dollars—money he didn't have at the time, but was able to pay off eventually due to his great success.

> "The beautiful thing about learning is that nobody can take it from you."
> —B.B. King

MUSIC WAS HIS BRIDGE AND HIS PASSION

Through the many challenges and obstacles King faced, the words of his old teacher stayed with him, inspiring him to try to set a good example for those who looked up to him. He always performed in a tuxedo, saying that he wanted to look his best. Even before he quit smoking, he would never smoke or drink on stage. The moral code he lived by was unusual among blues musicians, most of whom played hard—both in terms of their music and their lives.

King wasn't without moral failings, and his lyrics attest to that. But no one could ever question his commitment to his music. Music was B.B. King's passion, and he was willing to sacrifice much for it. How many people do you know who would run into a burning building to retrieve a piece of wood? Maybe to save a family member, a child, or even a beloved pet—but an instrument? That image is the essence of a passionate person.

> B.B. King didn't just create great music and a better life for himself. I believe he was one of many artists whose music helped to bridge the huge racial divide in our society.

As often happens, King's passion has inspired many others. He's influenced nearly every musician in the industry today, as well as world leaders. He holds six honorary doctorates; he was awarded the Polar Music Prize by the queen and king of Sweden; he's even performed with U2. (I thought that was cool.) So, even if you're thinking you don't like the blues, you should at least check out B.B. King and see what it is that gained him the admiration of so many.

I think it's amazing that so many musicians and other artists have had a lot to do with the racial integration of our culture. Although they faced a great deal of prejudice and discrimination, many African American artists had an "in" with mainstream white culture because of the art they passionately created. B.B. King didn't just create great music and a better life for himself. I believe he was one of many artists whose music helped to bridge the huge racial divide in our society.

Louis Armstrong, that father of jazz, was another revolutionary and passionate artist whose music helped tear down walls of racism and build bridges of understanding. Years before B.B. King, Armstrong was performing in segregated venues and gained massive accolades for his new style of music. His friendships with many of the big movie stars and other musicians of the day brought even more credibility to his craft. Armstrong is known not only as a groundbreaking musician but also as a civil rights hero. His musical excellence and passion gained him access and influence, allowing him to speak up and help lead efforts toward equality.

Sometimes the pursuit of your passion and the execution of it with excellence will buy you a seat at a table where you normally wouldn't have been invited. And sometimes, people will listen to what you have to say just because of your reputation as a passionate person.

Music has the ability to stir us and help us see things differently. Music may even be a tool God uses to help you uncover your passion—even if music itself is not one of your passions. Some people

B.B. King (Photo courtesy www.bbking.com)

have suggested that dedicating your life to making music or art is trivial or even irresponsible in a world where there is so much suffering—but I disagree. I think those who are talented and passionate about creating music and art provide a gift to the rest of us by putting words, melodies, and pictures to the events, struggles, and stories of our lives. God is the Creator—and he enables us to create as a reflection of him.

LOSE YOUR COOL, DISCOVER YOUR PASSION

Is there a song that is significant to you? Maybe the lyrics have spoken to your heart in a way that really moved or inspired you? If so, write the lyrics below.

The Psalms are the Bible's songbook, and many of them express people's deepest thoughts. Read Psalm 139. How does this song express your heart? Was there something you read that made you think, "Yes, that's how I feel"?

Do you think it was foolish, youthful passion that caused B.B. King to run into the building to save his guitar? Can you think of examples where a rash decision in a moment of passion can lead to disaster?

Have you ever made a split-second decision you regretted later?

What role do you think experience plays in making wise choices when faced with a decision in a moment of crisis? How do our values, standards, and commitments impact those decisions? How can our passion drive those decisions?

||||| FINDING INSPIRATION ||||||||||||||

I have "met" many great people—both current and past—by reading their stories. I often find inspiration from the courage and passion of other people. My friends, the Harris brothers, suggest that we need to be careful about the company we keep as we try to live a life pleasing to God. One way they recommend doing that is by being careful about the influences we put into our minds through the books we read and movies we watch. What you take in does impact who you become. So surround yourself with people who will bring you up—inspiring you to pursue God and to live in a way that pleases him. Choose literature, books, and music that draw you closer to the heart of God and help preserve your purity.

I'd encourage you to pick up biographies of both contemporary and historical figures. Study what made those people tick, what motivated them, and what they were passionate about. Let God speak to you through the lives of others. Some of my favorite biographies and autobiographies include *The Diary of Frederick Douglass*, *Of Beetles and Angels* by Mawi Asgedom, *The Hiding Place* by Corrie ten Boom (and its sequel, *Tramp for the Lord*), *Rosa Parks: My Story*, *Four Souls* by Jedd Medefind, *Touchdown Alexander* by Shaun Alexander, *Iqbal* by Francesco D'Adamo and Ann Leonori, and *No More Victims* by Frank Peretti. I've also enjoyed reading the sermons and speeches of Dr. Martin Luther King Jr.

I like to "interview" people I meet and find out about their lives. I bet there are some amazing stories in your neighborhood, school, and church. I've included a couple of interviews in this book to show how you can explore ideas with someone you respect. This is a great way to cultivate a mentoring relationship with someone.

Another place to explore stories of people who have made an impact on our world is The Academy of Achievement. Check it out online at www.achievement.org.

A CONVERSATION WITH JON FOREMAN

When I was in Los Angeles speaking at an event for students, I had the opportunity to sit down with my friend and mentor, Jon Foreman—the lead singer, guitarist, and cofounder of the band Switchfoot. I asked Jon a few questions about passion, and he graciously allowed me to take down his responses and share them with you in this book.

Zach: First of all, what is passion?

Jon: When I think of passion, I think of suffering and the folks who have died for something; I feel like they have a deeper sort of passion than anything I've experienced. It's one thing to say you're passionate about Led Zeppelin in junior high when everyone hates Led Zeppelin. But a true, deeper passion is being willing to suffer for something.

Zach: Who do you think exhibits passion?

Jon: There's a passage in the New Testament that includes a list of patriots, and hopers, and dreamers of times gone by who never got to see their dreams come true, never got to see the Promised Land. [Check out Hebrews 11 to see the passage Jon is talking about.] That is the first thing that comes to mind—the Abrahams of the world who were part of a dream much bigger than themselves.

Zach: Who is someone who exhibits a passion that is destructive, or maybe someone who was well intentioned, but let it get out of hand? Could you talk about that?

Jon: Absolutely (laughs). Go to any Little League game, and there's a chance you might see a few parents with some misdirected passion. We want to feel like our blood is tied to something bigger than ourselves; that's a genuine human desire—that's a great thing. But when that's misguided, it can lead to a lot of dangerous situations where passion is bringing us backward. You look at suicide bombings or even an overly intense patriotism that would make a nation decide they are somehow better than others. Suddenly you've got Hitler—sure, he had a lot of passion. So absolutely, like many of the other human attributes, passion can be a double-edged sword.

Zach: What are you passionate about?

Jon: When you use the word *passion*, it's like the word *love*—which has such a wide variety of hues and tones. C.S. Lewis talks about the "four loves." You know...you love your mom, you love asparagus, you love your high school football team, and you love the smell of the ocean. There's the "familiar love" and the "agape love," but what is the best love? In *The Four Loves* Lewis describes that while writing the book, he tried to put them in a hierarchy—but he found that all of these loves are tied together.

In our Western world we like to compartmentalize, which can tend to oversimplify things. For example the pursuit of holiness cannot leave out justice. Maintain a passion for your hometown ball team without forgetting the homeless who sleep downtown outside the stadium. Martin Luther King Jr. talked a lot about how we rise or fall as a society together. He said, "I can never be what I ought to be until you are what you ought to be, and you can never be what you ought to be until I am what I ought to be. This is the interrelated structure of reality."

So in this context I am passionate about my family, the smell of the sea, the hope I see in the eyes of a child, the smell of a freshly cut lemon, and a Creator who holds all of these in tension.

BILLY & PAUL

||||| **RUNNING TOWARD DESTINY** ||||||||||||||

"I would run five or ten miles on weekends to get away from everybody else," Billy Mills recalls. "And I cried. I'd be crying while I was running. A half-blood and an orphan—you couldn't get much lonelier than that."[1]

Billy Mills was born in South Dakota and grew up on the Pine Ridge Indian reservation. Like many other kids on the reservation, Billy grew up in poverty. But his situation was even more difficult, because both his parents died while he was still quite young. His mom died when he was seven, and his dad died when he was twelve.

On top of being without parents and dealing with poverty, Billy also had to battle racial prejudice. Because he was part Lakota and part Caucasian, both Indians on the reservation and the whites in the area treated him as an outsider. Although Billy's given Lakota name is *Makata Taka Hela* (which means "respects the earth"), Billy himself was often treated with disrespect. "Neither of those two cultures really allowed me to participate," he remembers. "Often I felt different, almost every day of my life, like [I didn't] belong."

Of course, as a child, Billy was heartbroken and distraught over not fitting in. But he always remembered something his dad had once said to him. One day his dad put his arms around Billy and told him, "You have broken wings...find your dream, for only values and virtues can heal you." He also said, "If you ever find that passion, it leads you down a path to a destiny."[2]

Billy started running at a young age and discovered he was pretty good at it. He decided to channel his desire and talent for running into something productive. He began running competitively during high school and broke several records. He did so well that he received an athletic scholarship to the University of Kansas.

HITTING HIS STRIDE

After completing college Billy was commissioned as a lieutenant in the United States Marine Corps. This was, it seems, where Billy really found himself. He said, "All my life I felt like I didn't belong. The Marine Corps said 'You belong.'"[3]

"Often I felt different, almost every day of my life."—Billy Mills

He continued to run, training with renewed confidence and discipline by running about 100 miles a week. His hard work paid off when he qualified to run in the 1964 Olympics. As usual there was a lot of hype leading up to the Olympics. The experts agreed that Billy's event, the 10,000 meter run, was likely to be a shootout between two runners: Mohammed Gammoudi of Tunisia and the Australian Ron Clarke. Billy was a supposed nonfactor. But what actually happened was quite different. Here's how the play-by-play might have gone:

Bang! The starting gun goes off and the runners leave their marks with determination to win. They have 25 laps ahead of them— that's 10,000 meters. Lap one goes by. Lap two. Three. Four. At lap five it's far too early to call. Six. Lap after lap, Billy Mills stays right up there with Clarke. Gammoudi is right behind the two leaders, who are both built more like tanks than runners. Lap 10, 15, 20—and the three runners continue to pull away from the pack. By the final lap the only ones who are a factor are Gammoudi, Clarke, and America's Billy Mills. Suddenly, Gammoudi stretches his arms out between Mills and Clarke and shoves them to the side. The crowd screams, and somehow Billy controls himself and refrains from punching Gammoudi. Gammoudi takes the lead, with Clarke right behind—but Mills has dropped back a couple of feet, and there's only one turn to go before the home stretch. The three runners are all sweating and panting and running as fast as they can after nearly six miles. And now American Billy Mills is gaining ground. As they reach the finish line, Billy leans forward—and he makes it! A huge smile comes across Billy's face, and rightfully so—not only is he the first Native American and the first U.S. Marine ever to win a gold medal in this event, he's the first American ever to win gold at this event!

Billy Mills's victory in 1964 is still considered one of the most fantastic upsets in Olympic history. But many people don't know that Billy almost didn't make it to the Olympic Games that year. In fact Billy contemplated suicide while he was in college. You see, one day a picture was being taken of the college track team. Billy was an All-American runner, but because he was dark-skinned, he was asked to step aside for the picture. This, on top of many other things, nearly sent Billy over the edge. He was sitting in his hotel room after the picture, and he decided he'd had enough. He was ready to jump out the window and end it all. This is what happened next, in his own words: "So I'm ready to jump. And I heard, not through my ears, but through my skin, 'Don't.' It was my dad's voice." And because Billy chose not to jump, because he heard and listened to his dad's voice, he went on to do significant things.

Billy Mills capturing the gold medal in Japan. Photo courtesy of www.indianyouth.org

SHAMELESS EXPLOITATION

As I've mentioned before, I love a good story—especially an inspiring one like Billy Mills's. And I also love stories where you think there's an obvious crescendo leading up to a big moment—and yet that moment is not the ultimate apex of the story. That's kind of how it is with Billy Mills—the Olympic gold medal wasn't the big deal. What Billy did later in life was.

What Billy Mills did in the 1964 Olympics was big—becoming the first American to ever win a gold medal in his event. But he didn't stop there. He went on and wrote books to share his years of insight and wisdom with people. He founded an organization to encourage Native American youth, and he speaks around the country. I think it's safe to say that the most significant work Billy Mills did began *after* he won the gold medal.

Actor Paul Newman's story is similar in many ways. I'm writing this chapter just days after Newman's death. Although Paul Newman is famous all over the world for his acting, he's also well known for something else that's even more important: Caring for people. You might think that the pinnacle of Paul Newman's story would see him standing on stage and receiving awards. But the real pinnacle, as was the case with Billy Mills, is found in what Newman decided to do with his life and fame outside of his acting career.

Paul Newman's food company, which he originally started as a joke, has one of my favorite mottos. The motto states the products are used for "Shameless Exploitation in Pursuit of the Common Good." I love that line because, while many other companies exploit their associations with charities to help them make even more money, Newman chose to exploit his own popularity for charities.

Newman's Own foods was making all-natural products long before "organic" was considered haute cuisine. One of the most amazing things about the business, though, is that Newman gave away *all* the profits from the sale of his foods. Not 10 percent of his profits—although that would have been generous. Not 50 percent—which others would have said was bad business. But 100 percent. This amazes me. And not only that, but Newman's Own food products are really great quality, and all natural. (My favorites are the "Hint O Mint Newman-Os" and the Concord Grape Juice—but not together!)

Paul Newman was one of the most brilliant business minds of our generation. Newman's Own has given away almost $250 million to improve the lives of others. He founded many great organizations such as Hole in the Wall Camps, which offers free summer camps for children with life-threatening illnesses. This offers a fun camp experience to kids who would not be able to go to most other camps because of the special care these kids need.

> You can do something small that makes a real difference, that really changes someone's life—and that's very significant. But it's also possible to do something big that really doesn't make any difference in the world.

Actress Sophia Loren expressed perfectly my own sentiments about the death of this mountain of a man when she said: "When such important personalities die, one despairs and thinks that, little by little, all the greats are disappearing." But his family continues his legacy of philanthropy by keeping alive Newman's Own. (Lucky for me and my love of Newman-Os!)

Many people don't know that Mr. Newman was an avid race car driver. He'd been looking for a sport he could compete in, and while filming a movie, he decided race cars were his thing. In 1995 he actually was a part of the winning team in a 24-hour endurance race at Daytona. He was 70 years old at that time. Someone once said that passion is wasted on the young, but Newman surely stayed passionate about racing—and about life—well into his 70s. NASCAR racer Tony Stewart said, "We connected as racers, but Paul's ideas of what we should do for charity is what really resonated with me the most."

Paul Newman used his name and face on the products to make the world a better place. If you've read my book *Be the Change*, you've read about this idea of "influence as currency." Newman discovered a cause he grew to care deeply about (more like *multiple* causes) and decided to do something to make a difference. He understood that the influence he'd amassed as an actor could be exchanged like currency to help others.

One thing I find amazing is that Paul Newman not only did big things to change the world in a corporate setting, he also did things on a personal level. He once flew to Great Britain to put on a show as a clown for sick children and children with disabilities. This world famous actor went to Europe to clown around for some kids—and he did it just four years before his death! Paul Newman dedicated years of his life to making the world a better place and to helping people in need.

BIG OR SIGNIFICANT?

I was talking with a friend recently who told me she thought the whole "ending slavery thing" that I work on is cool. I said something like, "I don't really care if anyone remembers my efforts or my campaign—what I really want is for people to see that my generation put aside our differences, said 'This is not ok,' and came together to end slavery—that we abolished slavery by working together. That's what matters." Then she said something that struck me, "It's always the people who do big or significant things that are remembered after they die; so you'll probably be remembered."

First of all, that was very kind of her to say. And I was especially struck by the way she talked about doing things that are big or significant. It's important to realize that those two words don't always go together. Something doesn't have to be big for it to be significant. You can do something small that makes a real difference, that really changes someone's life—and that's very significant. But it's also possible to do something big that really doesn't make any difference in the world.

For example let's say you are a world-class runner. After you finish your running career, you have a choice. You can retire and sit on your porch drinking lemonade and showing off your gold medal whenever anyone comes by. Or, you can be like Billy Mills and use the fame and influence you've gained to improve the world.

Or, what about Paul Newman? He would have been viewed as a great success for his acting alone, even if he'd never spoken publicly when his film career was done. But instead he chose to use his influence on behalf of those less fortunate—and much of what he did to help others was small gestures that will never even be known about by most of us. Before his death Newman said that he really wanted his legacy to be his camps. Not all his awards or his film credits, but the camps for kids who otherwise would have been left out.

You don't have to do something *big* in order to make a *significant* difference.

LOSE YOUR COOL, DISCOVER YOUR PASSION

What did running provide for Billy Mills?

Do you think he'd have discovered his passion for running if it didn't come out of necessity?

It amazes me when I hear teenagers who have already given up on the possibility of making a difference. Maybe they've lost interest because something didn't go quite right or cashed it in because someone didn't like their ideas. How is Billy's approach to life different?

What does the life of Paul Newman show us about pursuing different interests and passions, not letting someone box us in and force us to be who they think we should be?

Hebrews 12:1 says "Therefore, since we are surrounded by such a great cloud of witnesses, let us throw off everything that hinders and the sin that so easily entangles, and let us *run* with *perseverance* the race marked out for us" (emphasis mine). How can we apply this verse when it comes to pursuing our passions?

Is there someone in your life whom others are trying to keep down? It might be because of that person's race, family, or position in the pecking order at school. What can you do to encourage such people that God has a plan for their lives? (What if that person is the next Billy Mills or Paul Newman, but he or she is being held down by those who say it can't be done? Maybe you're the one holding that person down.)

When you are in crisis or having a difficult time, what voices do you listen to? Read James 1:5 for some advice about whom we should listen to first. How can you discern which voices in your life are for your good and consistent with God's voice?

What small things have you done or successes have you had that God can make into something significant? Can you see any of them developing into a passion?

||||| BIG OR SIGNIFICANT? |||||||||||

Sometimes we think that—in order to make a difference, in order to make our passions known, in order to follow God—we have to do something big. We think we have to discover the cure to some disease, or get on national television to spread the word about ending some social problem, or "convert" hundreds of people—but this is not ALWAYS the case. All these things can be very important and admirable, and they can be useful strategies to bring change. If you've gotten on national TV, or made some scientific breakthrough, or told a bunch of people about Jesus, then that's great—but don't believe that everything you do has to be BIG. That just isn't true.

The guy back home donating cash or the girl who's writing letters to help the cause of the oppressed is seeking justice just as much as the person who founded an international relief agency. None of them could make a difference without one another. And you don't have to get on national TV to spread the word about the issue you care about. You can have an impact by using your influence to speak out to all those contacts in your cell phone and all those friends on Facebook.

I'd encourage you to check out the movie *Running Brave* to find out more about Billy Mills and how he has used his influence to help others. (You can find the film at www.indianyouth.org.)

In the film there's an interesting scene that I think sums up the lives of people like Billy Mills and Paul Newman—and I hope your own life, too. In that scene Billy's wife, Pat, asks him if he really intends to run in the Olympics.

"Sure," he responds. "Why?"

"Oh, because everyone here says they'll do things and never does them. You're really doing something."

Let's be a generation that does something.

LEIPZIG

||||| WE ARE THE PEOPLE |||||||||||||

It is white like a dream. The rows of white pews mirror the white columns, which mirror the white tile floor. At the front is a white altar bearing a crucifix. In the middle of the center aisle is a small metal tree with a candle on the end of each branch.

This is the Church of St. Nikolai in Leipzig—a town in the Eastern part of Germany. I visited this church during the summer of 2008, when I went to Germany for an international gathering for young people of faith. At that conference I met amazing people from all around the world and was very encouraged by what God is doing through kids of all nationalities. I also had the opportunity to learn a little about the dark history of the town, as well as the resilient people who took a stand for justice there by holding prayer meetings. Here's how the story goes.

The year was 1989. The month, September. At this time Germany was divided into two independent countries. Basically, West Germany was a thriving place, looking much like any prosperous nation. But in East Germany, where the town of Leipzig was located, the common people were languishing. The Communist government of East Germany acted as if it were the people's voice. But the residents of Leipzig responded with a peaceful revolution whose motto was, "We *are* the people." Many of the people who protested were imprisoned because it was illegal to protest at all—even peacefully.

PEACEFUL REVOLUTION

The pastor (or parson) of the Church of St. Nikolai at the time was a man named Christian Führer. I had the chance to hear him speak on my trip to Germany. He talked about how the many people who had protested against Communist rule had been imprisoned, because even peaceful protest was illegal. Yet tension was growing, and the movement for change in East Germany, which was being called the Peaceful Revolution, was gaining momentum.

> I imagined what it would have been like to march and sing with these freedom seekers.

At the center of all this conflict and excitement was the Berlin Wall, which kept East and West Germany separate. It was a physical wall that had been built back in 1961. The wall cut off all transportation between East and West Germany. Over the years many people tried to escape from the East to the West, and 192 people were killed trying to break through. The wall was not only a physical barrier; it was also a psychological barrier and a symbol of the control and intimidation tactics of the Communists. The wall stood for oppression and division. It needed to be torn down.

Back in Leipzig—about 150 kilometers from Berlin—Parson Führer had an idea. He and all the people of the Church of St. Nikolai began holding peaceful prayer meetings every week. These gatherings, called *Montagsdemonstrationen* (Monday Demonstrations), were powered not by guns, tanks, or airplanes, but by candles and prayers of peace.

This soft-spoken pastor and the people who met in his pristine white chapel caused quite a commotion. The prayer meetings were investigated by Communist officials, who actually tried to break up a couple of the meetings. They challenged Führer: "You are holding a demonstration!" to which he replied, "It is not a demonstration, it's just a prayer meeting." And truly, it was.

By October 9, 1989—just a few weeks after the prayer vigils had begun—the crowd at the church swelled to 70,000 (in a city of 500,000). Two weeks later there were more than 300,000 people. Just imagine, for a second, what it must have been like for the guards and security forces on special watch. Here was a vast army of people—walking, carrying candles, and praying. The Communist army hadn't received orders from East Berlin to fire on the crowd, so they stood by. What could have been a massacre was instead a powerful nonviolent demonstration of the solidarity of the people and their longing for freedom and unity.

WEAPONS NOT OF THIS WORLD

When Parson Führer spoke about these events, he said something like this about the Communists' response to the people's revolution. "If we came in tanks, they were prepared. If we came with guns, they were prepared. If we came with planes, they were prepared. The only thing they weren't prepared for was thousands of people carrying candles and singing hymns." These demonstrations marked the beginning of the end of the Communist regime in East Germany and the division between East and West. Within a short time the Berlin Wall would fall.

So there I stood, two decades later, in this beautiful white cathedral, looking at the pristine white candles flickering on the branches. I imagined what it would have been like to march and sing with these freedom seekers. Just a few days earlier, I'd stood on the exact spot where the Berlin Wall had once towered and intimidated, and then walked from what would have been the East to the West. I remember talking with my friends on the trip about our shared faith in God and our love for freedom.

The wall stood for oppression and division. It needed to be torn down.

While I was in Germany, I met some real characters—including some crazy, off-the-wall, bigger-than-life believers in Jesus. But I also met some quiet, shy, "let me stay in the background" followers of Christ. I think we have the tendency to value those who are most visible, most charismatic. But I always wonder what work God is preparing in the hearts of the quieter, less noticed people.

Christian Führer didn't have a big plan. He wasn't seeking worldwide fame. He wasn't looking to build a legacy for himself or for the Church of St. Nikolai. He was simply doing what he knew would make a difference in a desperate time—drawing God's people together to pray. The rest was up to God. And the results were world changing.

LOSE YOUR COOL, DISCOVER YOUR PASSION

It seems that, when God's people are being crushed, God plants a passion for freedom and survival. Where have you seen this in Scripture? Where have you seen it in history?

What role do you think desperation played in Christian Führer and his church's turning to prayer?

The movement grew quickly in Leipzig and the costs were great. People could have lost their lives just by showing up at the prayer meeting. What kind of situation would move you to that kind of passionate and brave pursuit?

Sometimes we think "passionate" means loud. How can Godly passion be manifested in quieter people or in quiet acts?

If you've been asked to do something behind the scenes rather than being chosen for the visible role, how did that make you feel?

Read Philippians 2:3. How do you think this verse relates to the qualifications of a passionate leader?

AWAKENING A NEW PASSION

Leipzig is known as the "city of music," because it is the birthplace of Bach, Mendelssohn, Schumann, and Wagner. When in Germany I was able to visit the church where Bach played. I remember looking up at the massive organ balcony and imagining what it must have been like to hear the great composer play to people filling the pews.

I was thinking recently about how, when many of these great composers came onto the scene, what they were doing was groundbreaking and revolutionary—and sometimes it wasn't all that popular. In our society today many people—especially teens—turn up their noses at new things or unfamiliar things. A lot of my peers are quick to offer their opinions about what they hate. I'll hear another student say, "I hate Thai food" or "I hate skiing"—and then, when prodded, admit he's never really tried the things he hates. There are people who say, "I hate (fill in type of music)"—when, in reality, they've never listened to this music or given it a fair chance. In fact I think a lot of us tend to talk a lot more about what we don't like, what annoys us, what we would never try, than about the things we really do like. But would you rather be around cynical people who talk continually about what they hate or people who find joy in the small things?

The most passionate people I know enjoy and appreciate a wide variety of things—in fact, such people rarely talk about how much they hate things that are inconsequential. I think being open to trying something new is one mark of a passionate person. If you're passionate about life, you probably won't say, "I can't stand..." about something you've never tried before. Now, of course, I'm not talking about trying damaging or immoral things; I'm talking about trying something new that will expand your horizons and interests.

Maybe we can be a little more adventurous—try some new things. Take up a new hobby, try new food, learn a new language, explore art or history, listen to a new kind of music—find a way to appreciate experiences that others love. It may help you see the world differently. It may even be a way for God to awaken a new passion in you.

Let me get you started on that adventure by recommending some music that might not already be in your iPod:

The Passion Playlist

Folk	Jon Foreman's four solo albums: *Fall, Winter, Spring,* and *Summer*
Country	Johnny Cash: Any of his *American Recordings*
Hip Hop/ Rap	The Washington Projects: *Commanders of the Resistance*
Alternative	Edison Glass: *A Burn or a Shiver* and *Time Is Fiction*

Jazz	Charlie Peacock: *Love Press Ex-Curio* and *The Arc of the Circle*; John Coltrane: *Ballads*
Blues	Jonny Lang: *Turn Around*
Classical	Vivaldi: *The Four Seasons*; Beethoven: "Moonlight Sonata," "Piano Trio in G"

Email me your ideas for other music that inspires you at loseyourcool@gmail.com.

Log in to www.loseyourcoolbook.com and download a free song that will get you thinking and expand your musical horizons!

A CONVERSATION WITH WESS STAFFORD

I recently sat down with Wess Stafford, president of Compassion International, a child development agency best known for its sponsorship of children around the world. Dr. Stafford spent his own childhood at a missionary school in Africa where he was beaten and abused frequently. But he persevered through that and now works to help children who are going through some of the same things he saw and experienced as a child. Dr. Stafford has become a friend and mentor to me, and I was glad to have the chance to ask him a few questions about passion...

Zach: How would you define the word *passion* as it relates to the word *compassion*?

Wess: Well, first let's look at the word *compassion*. "Com" is the first part; it means "with." But what does the "passion" part mean? Well, I thought it had to mean "warm heart," "generous spirit," or "tender heart." Here's the shocker: *Passion* actually means "to suffer." And so what Jesus was saying in Luke 6:36 ["You must be compassionate, just as your Father is compassionate" (NLT)] was basically like everything else he taught: "I'm asking you to go outside of your culture, outside of your generation; I'm asking you to do something really upstream and outside of the norm. I'm asking you, not to solve all the problems of everyone in the world, but to do something even more courageous and more demanding. I'm asking you to actually suffer with those who suffer. I'm asking you to be weak with those who are weak, and to cry with those who cry."

And we are told in the Scriptures 12 times that Jesus was moved with compassion; and every time he was moved with compassion, he did something. He felt this, and then he did something. The word in Greek is a cool word; it's a long word that basically means a churning in your stomach. You are really feeling something. You don't just see it and think, "Oh, that's sad." That's pity. But passion is when you feel it and you say, "Argh! I have to do something about this!" That's the word that the Greek playwrights would use when they wanted to describe a warhorse. You know, these big, powerful animals covered in armor and trained for battle? When a warhorse is on the hill, anticipating going into battle, it literally trembles in anticipation. The word used to describe that emotional, in-your-gut anticipation is *compassion*.

So there are two parts: The first is that you literally feel the suffering of other people, and the other is that you literally feel compelled to leap in and do something about it. Compassion is the opposite of complacency.

As you often say, Zach, it's not enough to just feel bad about slavery or other injustices in the world. That does nobody any good; just feeling bad never helped anyone. That's what I hear you crying out for your generation, "Come on, let's not let ourselves get disarmed by comfort and the unimportant stuff." I think you guys have it right: There are a lot of things to be interested in, but only a handful to be passionate about—so choose them wisely.

When you see people being passionate about the wrong things, it's really sad. I think failure for a Christian is to succeed at something that doesn't really matter. A lot of people, when they get to my age, hit what they call a midlife crisis. Suddenly you get midway through your life, and you look at what you've accomplished, and you say, "Is this really all there is?" Building a career is like climbing up a ladder, but some people get to the top and realize their ladder is leaning against the wrong wall. It's a pointless, stupid wall; all they did was make money. Or they made money and the bottom line of what they did was making money for other people. So a lot of people get to this point of their life and decide they need to move from "success" to "significance." And significance means, "I gotta matter! I gotta do something that matters!"

Zach: Do you think you have to experience a certain amount of pain to feel passionate or compassionate?
Wess: Well, you did, and I did. I think you'll find that most people who are really passionate about something have a powerful reason or story about why they are passionate. I don't think it's fair to say that you "have to" suffer. Because I believe the Holy Spirit can stir up a person from the midst of the comfort of suburbia to care about the poor. So I think it would be interesting to see, as you are talking to people, why they got passionate about something. But I would guess that those people who have absolutely given themselves to a cause like I have—my cause being the poor and children—I think that if you dig deep enough, you will often find most of them have a great reason for that passion.

I think any person who has a good heart, is open to the Holy Spirit, and is willing to learn can still find that passion. What is it that the founder of World Vision, Bob Pierce, used to say? "Let my heart be broken by the things that break the heart of God." For him it was poverty, but, as you say, there are several different things to be passionate about: The fact that people don't hear the gospel; the fact that kids suffer in broken family situations, the fact that kids get sucked away into drugs, and even the fact that kids get sucked into the whole culture of, "It's all about being beautiful outside, who cares what's inside." All those are traps Satan uses to separate people from God. Satan attacks what God loves most, humans. God is passionate about us. One of the major weapons Satan uses against humans, besides poverty, is comfort. He studies the world, and says, "Well, over here in Africa, I'll use poverty, and over here in America, well, they already have all the resources; I'll do it with comfort. They'll get so focused on their comfort and pointless *stuff* that God is out of their frame of reference." What do you think? [Wait... he's asking me a question!?] Do you think it takes a powerful experience to generate passion?

Zach: Well, I don't think it takes a revelation or a "mountain top" experience. I mean, that's usually what people think it takes, but...
Wess: Right, and if it doesn't happen, then they don't feel like they've got something.

Zach: Right. I think it's really funny that people pray—I mean, I think it's good that people pray—but it's funny when they pray, "Should I get involved in this cause?" And then they say, "I'm not sure if God really wants me to help these people, or maybe I should help over here." Bottom line: It's never wrong to serve the poor. It's ironic, like they're waiting for a sign from God, but the existence of people who are hurting and the biblical mandate to "seek justice" should be enough.
Wess: I've had that experience, too. Sometimes I'm at a Compassion International dinner, and we're asking people if they want to help out by paying a small amount to sponsor, and the people say, "Well, let me pray about this." I know what God's gonna say. He's not gonna

say, "No, you can't afford this. No, I don't care about the children. Poverty's not a big deal."

Zach: (laughs)
Wess: If you pray about it, God'll say yes.

Zach: Who is the most passionate person you've ever known or known about, and what made that person that way?

> "I think failure for a Christian is to succeed at something that doesn't really matter."
> —Dr. Wess Stafford

Wess: My dad. We tend to think of passionate people as displaying it really well outwardly. And that's true of some passionate people. But my father felt things as deeply as I do. He never could describe it in words, but he lived it out. When he died, people came and talked to me, and I suddenly realized all these things he had been doing. One guy came to me and said, "You might not know this, but your dad gave me his truck. I'd lost my job, and your dad just drove his truck into my yard, told me I could have it, and walked home." My dad never told me that. This is why, I think, that when we get to heaven, the people we thought were heroes, aren't; because the real measure of passion is deep down inside, and only God can measure that.

I live just moments above the tear level. If I take a moment and stop and ponder, I am reduced to tears. The tears would be one of two things. They could be tears of sadness, because of the pain in the world, because I lost half of my boyhood friends. Or they could be tears of great joy. Just to be a part of the leadership of an organization like Compassion International sometimes brings me to tears; it's amazing.

I heard about a very wealthy family—and I'm talking extreme wealth here—who went with a group of people to an exclusive resort community in a tropical destination. Their children were with them as the group was checking in. The adults entered the hotel with wide eyes because of the lush beauty and opulence that surrounded them.

One adult commented, "This is a really nice hotel." To which one of the children answered, a bit surprised, "All hotels are nice."

No, all hotels that *you've* been to are nice. Everything you've experienced because you were blessed to grow up in a privileged setting has been "nice." This family and its children are like America. Even our worst poverty would seem like wealth to many people-groups around the world. But because we've only been exposed to our surroundings, we don't understand—we don't feel compassion for—those in other situations that are much less pleasant, clean, and hopeful than ours. Those who live every day in slavery, or are without clean water, or are dying of starvation.

But when we experience pain of some kind, we start to understand how much others might hurt in their circumstances. If we've lost a good friend, or a loved one has died, or our parents divorced, or we've been really sick, or we've moved away from all our friends and had to start over again, maybe we can grasp the suffering of others a little better. I don't think it's absolutely necessary for us to go through an intense pain like those I just mentioned, but it may be easier for us to step into someone else's suffering if we've been close to it ourselves, if we've felt pain and even despair. I say, don't let those painful experiences go to waste. God likely wants to use your scars and your sensitivity to support others, because you "get it." You've been there.

For those who haven't been there—congratulations. You're one of the few. But if you live long enough in this fallen world, you'll get your turn. Jesus promised it. Did you know that? [Actually, I did know it—my dad says, jokingly, that it's his least favorite promise in the Bible: "In this world you will have trouble" (or tribulation). Not "maybe," not "most of you." He said, "You *will* have trouble." But then Jesus says, "Be of good cheer; I have overcome the world."]

We can be part of helping others overcome hurting, but first we need to understand their pain.

||||| **HEARING** |||||||||||||

Okay, picture this: A friend comes up to you and exclaims, "Dude! I was out in my yard last night when I heard this voice from God telling me to go put on armor and fight for my country!" Would that seem just a little crazy to you? Well, someone actually did experience this crazy "voice from God"—in fact, it was a 13-year-old girl named Jehanne (zhawn). And this is her story.

Jehanne grew up in France in a small village called Domremy. At an early age, as a committed Catholic, she was taught by her mother to say her prayers. Jehanne also learned to sew and spin on a spinning wheel and could soon spin as well as any woman in the village. From the door of her house, Jehanne could see a forested area called the Polled Wood. Legend said that a maiden who would do amazing things would come through the woods one day. Jehanne knew that legend, but she dismissed it, saying "I had no faith in that."

I'll let her tell you the next part of her story in her own words (translated from French to English):

> When I was thirteen I had a voice from God to help me govern myself. The first time, I was terrified. The voice came to me about noon: it was summer, and I was in my father's garden...There was

a great light all about...I saw it many times before I knew it was St. Michael [the archangel]...He was not alone, but...attended by heavenly angels...And when they left me, I wept, and I wished that they might have taken me with them...Above all, Saint Michael told me that I must be a good child, and that God would help me... He told me the pitiful state of the Kingdom of France. And he told me that I must go to [aid] the King of France...Twice and thrice a week the voice told me that I must depart and go into France...the voice told me that I would raise the siege before Orleans...And it told me to go to...[the] captain of the town, who would give me men to go with me. And I answered the voice [and said] that I was a poor girl and knew nothing of riding and warfare.[1]

Jehanne told no one about her visions at the time, because she was afraid her father would say she could not go. Her father had dreamt that Jehanne would run away with a band of soldiers. At the time, the French were being beaten badly by the English in a fight for independence. Everything the French did seemed to bring about defeat. Times were desperate. Jehanne believed she had to go—even against her family's will—because God had commanded it. So she devised a plan.

SETTING OUT

Jehanne visited her uncle, and he agreed to take her to Vaucouleurs—the town where she was supposed to meet the captain in her vision. When she got there, she immediately recognized the man she was supposed to meet, Captain Robert, even though she'd never seen him before. Once again the voices had given her direction. She went to Captain Robert and asked him to give her soldiers to help her on her quest. He rejected her twice before finally granting what she asked.

So Jehanne and her group of six men set out to help her nation in its time of need. To disguise herself young Jehanne wore men's clothes. (At the time it was considered dangerous and sacrilegious for a woman to wear "trousers.") She carried a sword Robert had given her—but otherwise she was unarmed. Jehanne and her men arrived in Chinon, where she went to see the French king in his castle. When she met King Charles, she walked directly up to him (as the voices had told her) and explained that God had told her she was the one who would bring France to victory over the English. The king was amazed and kept Jehanne in Chinon for several weeks where she was examined and questioned by his advisors. The king's men could see nothing but good coming from her efforts.

> "I would rather die than do something which I know to be a sin, or to be against God's will." —Jehanne

THE BATTLE BANNER

Jehanne had a banner made to carry into battle. The banner depicted God standing in the middle of a field of lilies while holding the world, with two angels standing on each side. The voice from God told her there would be a sword for her behind the altar in the church of Saint Catherine. The rusty sword was found by her people in that exact place. When the priests rubbed it, the rust fell right off. Jehanne said she loved the sword, but she "loved the banner forty times better than the sword. And when I went against the enemy I carried the banner myself, lest I kill [anyone]."[2]

She told King Charles God had given her four things to do: (1) Drive the English out of France, (2) bring King Charles to the town of Reims to be crowned and anointed, (3) rescue the Duke of Orleans from the English, (4) lead the siege on Orleans. The king immediately assigned young Jehanne to lead a campaign with 10,000–12,000 soldiers under her charge. Before leaving she sent a warning letter to the King of England, telling him the English army should leave France immediately or else be vanquished.

> "I am not afraid... I was born to do this." —Jehanne

Jehanne, the teenage commander, told all her soldiers to confess their sins to God and to ask for his protection in combat, "because, for sin, God will permit the loss of this war." On the day before the battle, she tied a message to an arrow that was shot into English lines. The gist of the message was, "Surrender now—or you will see defeat." She talked with the chaplain of her band and told him to stay close to her in the battle, because she would be wounded above her chest.

The next day Jehanne's army set out to take the fortress in Orleans, and the fighting began. The battle was intense, with swords clanging, horses neighing, battle cries, and the groans of the wounded and dying. When Jehanne got to the fortress, she set up a ladder against its outside wall. As she stood the ladder up, an archer took aim with his crossbow, and shot her in the throat. She survived the wound, though, and the French forced the English from the fort. Then Jehanne ordered her soldiers not to kill any more, saying it was enough that they had conquered the fortress.

BIG PROMISE AND VICTORIES

From the fort Jehanne sent a letter telling King Charles to meet her in Reims, where she would see him crowned. This was a huge promise, because she would have to win more battles to make her way to Reims. But she and her band bravely fought through, defeating each group of English soldiers they came across, and successfully made it to Reims, where King Charles accepted his crown.

Jehanne and her forces won many more battles and skirmishes, capturing towns and moving the French ahead. Along the way she still believed the voice of God was guiding her with messages that protected her men and miraculously brought victory. Once, when she disobeyed the messages by going into a specific battle, the French lost and Jehanne was wounded. But she healed within five days, and they moved on.

Word spread throughout France about this amazing girl who was known simply as, "the Maid." At one stop in a town along the way, she was told that all the girls in the town were gathering to pray for the life of a baby who had died. Jehanne decided to join them. Even though the baby had been in the ground for three days, they dug him up so they could pray for him. As Jehanne and the other girls were praying, the baby yawned, and the color returned to his face.

After that miracle the French raised a siege against the British in the town of Compiègne. Jehanne and her men where pushed back. As they retreated Jehanne was captured. She was held in the prison tower for four months. She thought constantly about jumping—first, because she couldn't bear to be held by her enemies, and second, because she had heard from the British that every man, woman, and child in the town of Compiègne was to be killed by fire or by the sword.

AN ESCAPE

Finally Jehanne jumped from the tower, survived the jump, and escaped. But she was later captured again and had to appear on trial before the British. She told her captors that, if they knew enough about her, they'd wish to be rid of her, because everything she did was done by divine revelation. She was questioned about hearing the voice of God and answered that she heard it every day. In fact, the voice had told her to answer her captors bravely, because God would guide her. She told them, "You say you are my judge. Take thought over what you are doing. For, truly, I am sent from God, and you are putting yourself in great danger." The guards asked if she wanted to wear women's clothes rather than the armor she'd been captured in. She said she would be glad to wear the dress if they would let her go, but if not, she was content with what she was wearing, since it pleased God for her to wear it.

She was on trial for several days. Her captors questioned her about everything from whether the angels who appeared to her had wings and hair to when God had said the French would achieve victory. Although she was still just a girl, Jehanne was unwavering, offering quick answers and rebuttals when asked foolish questions. She refused to speak about anything God had told her not to reveal, reminding them that God was her judge, not anyone on earth: "He is the king of heaven and earth."

She was told that, unless she signed a document stating that all the things she'd said and done were evil, she would be burned at the stake. At first, she signed it, but was then told by God that it was a wicked thing to do. So she renounced her signature, saying that if she must die, then she must die. Two days later Jehanne was tied to the stake. As she was engulfed in flames, her last words were, "Jesus, Jesus!"

CRAZY OR COMMITTED?

Jehanne's allegiance to God and her country led her to do some things that seemed crazy. Many "experts" today would say Jehanne was delusional or that she suffered from schizophrenia. That was not the case. She did the impossible because she believed and followed the voices sent by God. Divine duty compelled her to serve. Because she talked about things outside the realm of what people thought possible, many people—both then and now—view her as being crazy.

But just in case I was unclear, I do not think Jehanne was insane. She followed the voices God gave her, which seemed crazy to the world. And she's not the first or the last person to be thought crazy for following where God leads. The British abolitionist William Wilberforce, one of my heroes, was once accused of being a lunatic. He responded, "If to be feelingly alive...is to be a fanatic, then I am one of the most incurable fanatics permitted to be at large."[3]

Maybe there are people who think you're crazy because of your passion for something. Perhaps people make fun of you because of your faith or what you've chosen to do with your life—even (or especially) if it's the right thing to do. In fact, if you're following Jesus, many people will find your actions and words strange and definitely countercultural.

> "Act, and God will act." —Jehanne

WISE VOICES

Here are a couple of things we can learn from Jehanne's story. First, we need to be careful about which voices we listen to. We hear a lot of voices every day—the media, our parents, our teachers, our friends, and others. But we have a choice about which voices we take to heart and whose directions we live out. The people you choose to listen to will shape your thoughts about yourself, others, and your world, and will even influence your behavior.

When it comes to areas like media and entertainment, choose wisely. There are words and images that, once put into our minds, are really hard to get out. The lifestyles and attitudes lived out on the movie screen or sung about in song lyrics, can shape our values. This happens slowly—almost without our realizing it—as we become more accustomed to seeing and hearing things that, at one time, might have bothered us.

With friends, be careful who is influencing you and whose advice you're accepting. It's also important, if you're a Christian, to learn to recognize the voice of God in our lives. In order to do this, we must read God's Word—the Bible. Anything we do should line up with its teachings. Use God's voice as the measure to discern what other voices and influences you take in. Jehanne listened to and took heed of the voices God sent to her but did not allow the voices of her prosecutors to sway her from her convictions—a good example for us.

The second thing we can learn from Jehanne is the value of preparation. Jehanne didn't just go out and fight the British on her own. She had a community of people surrounding her—and a God who was on her side. In preparation for her largest battles, she and all her men fasted, prayed, and confessed their sins before engaging the enemy. In this way they were prepared because they'd humbled themselves and acknowledged that they couldn't secure the victory without God's help. So God came to their aid.

The only portrait Jehanne was known to have sat for can no longer be found. But this image of Jehanne and her famous banner is from Centre Historique des Archives Nationales, Paris, AE II 2490.

I love Jehanne because she is a great example of someone passionately committed to doing what is right regardless of the cost. It's not that she didn't know the cost or weigh it carefully. She did. But then she chose to do what God directed her to do anyway.

Oh, and if you've not guessed by now, Jehanne isn't the name this young woman is most widely known by among English speakers. The story you've just read is about the 17-year-old martyr most of us know as Saint Joan of Arc.

LOSE YOUR COOL, DISCOVER YOUR PASSION

Are there things you're passionate about that seem beyond your ability to address? Is there something you want to pursue in life that you are not equipped to do—at least not yet?

Many voices in the entertainment world encourage thinking that erodes godly principles like sexual purity, honoring our parents, keeping our language clean, avoiding coarse or crude joking, and being honest. On the other hand, God's voice, God's Word, tells us to hold onto these principles. Which voices will you listen to? Who do you listen to now? How do the voices you hear build up your faith, self-respect, and values? Are they equipping you for a positive future?

When you're facing difficult decisions, to whom do you go for advice and help? How do you know if the counsel you're receiving is wise? Why is it important to have confidence in the "voices" you're listening to?

Is there something you sense God asking you to explore or do? Has your sense about this been confirmed by others in your life?

Ask God to give you help and wisdom as you consider this issue. Reflect on James 1:5: "If any of you lacks *wisdom*, he should *ask God*, who gives generously to all without finding fault, and it will be given to him" (emphasis mine).

Is there someone you can trust who has experience in this area? Who might be able to give you advice?

|||||| JUJITSU KID ||||||||||||

It's an ordinary day in the suburbs as nine-year-old Drew Heredia walks down the street with his neighbor who is walking her dachshund. They just picked up the mail when the little dog is suddenly attacked by a large pit bull. The girl tries to save her dog, but the pit bull turns on her and begins attacking her, biting her shoulder. Drew grabs the dog and tries out a move he'd just learned briefly in his jujitsu class—the choke hold.

Drew wrapped his forearm around the dog's throat and pushed his free hand into the back of the powerful dog's neck. The pit bull, which had been moving around and bucking like a bull, was restrained. The little nine-year-old, whom his mom describes as a "passive, sweet boy," maintained the hold for at least 20 minutes until animal-control officials showed up on the scene, potentially saving the life of both his friend and her dog.

This young jujitsu kid didn't start out that day believing he'd end it as a hero. He simply did what he could with what he had. Teddy Roosevelt once talked about how sometimes a person has "greatness thrust upon him"—and Drew was one of those people. Like Joan of Arc, he was an unlikely hero. When the dog attacked, he could have run away to ensure his own safety. Instead, Drew stepped in when his friend was in danger and found the courage and strength needed to come to the rescue.

AKIANE & MAYA

||||| **THE BLESSING OF GOD** |||||||||||||

"I have been blessed by God. And if I'm blessed, there is one reason and one reason only, and that is to help others" A girl named Akiane (ah-kee-AH-nuh) Kramarik said these words when she was only nine years old. That was five years after she received her first vision from God.

Akiane was born at home in Illinois to a Lithuanian mother and an American father, both of whom were atheists. During her childhood her family went through mixed financial situations—some good, some bad—but for the most part their life together resembled that of any normal working-class family. At least, until Akiane was four years old, and she had the experience of being "taken to heaven." Here is how her mother tells the story in the book *Akiane: Her Life, Her Art, Her Poetry*:

> One morning when Akiane was four, she began sharing her visions of heaven with us. "Today I met God," Akiane whispered to me one morning. "What is God?" I was surprised to hear this. To me, God's name always sounded absurd and primitive. "God is light—warm and good. It knows everything and talks with me. It is my parent."

Akiane told of how she'd seen colors much more beautiful than those existing on earth, and even described how she'd met Jesus. This freaked out her parents, because there'd never been any talk of God, heaven, or an invisible realm in their household—and now here was four-year-old Akiane sharing about her time with Jesus. Her parents wrestled with this for a long time, trying to rationalize what she'd experienced. But they soon realized there was no rational explanation. Eventually Akiane led her parents to Christ.

Akiane Kramarik
(Courtesy of Art Akiane, LLC)

VISIONS OF BEAUTY

Akiane had other visions and felt inspired to draw. The pencil sketches she did when she was just starting out at age four are definitely better than anything I could do at 16. Her art progressed from the shades of gray expressed in graphite and charcoal to a world of color when her family gave her some oil pastels.

Her visions continued, and at times, she woke up in the middle of the night saying she had something to say or paint—and she would just paint the image in her head, or recite a poem her mother would write down. Her family remained constantly surprised by the words that came from Akiane's mouth and the pictures painted by her hands. She soon graduated from pastel to oil and acrylic, which she paints on large canvases. And they *are* huge—48 x 60 inches, or four feet by five feet. If you go online and check out the artwork on her website at www.artakiane.com, you probably won't believe that she painted these pieces when she was so young. But they have video of her painting as well as photographs and eyewitnesses. Akiane has always insisted God is the one who gives her the inspiration.

Akiane, who turns 15 in 2009, went on *Oprah* when she was nine years old. She says she was really nervous, but Oprah calmed her down and made her feel better. She handled the interview very well, and Oprah loved her painting *The Planted Eyes*, which depicts an African woman meant to represent the sufferings of the African race. Since then, Akiane and her work have been featured on TV, in magazines, and in newspapers around the world.

Akiane's art is incredibly emotive, and her work continues to amaze me. If you look at her paintings in chronological order from the time she was four to the present, you constantly wonder, "Can they get any better?" And then the next painting contains dimensions that stop you in your tracks.

> When asked, "Do you teach other children?" Akiane replied, "Sometimes. I simply teach them how to see."

Recently Akiane sat down at a piano and decided she'd like to learn to play. Before long, she was playing like an experienced pianist and composing her own pieces. God has given her the gift of creating beautiful things for all of us to enjoy.

DOES GOD STILL MOVE?

Like Joan of Arc, Akiane has faced controversy and criticism as she's pursued God's unique calling to her. People have claimed she's crazy for talking about God as a personal friend or claiming to have received visions from God in dreams. Others say she charges too much for her paintings (one of which recently sold for $1 million). Yet she continues to use her gifts not only to tell the stories of the voiceless, but also to support them by giving much of the profits from her artwork to good causes, such as a project that provides support to children living in the dumps of Lithuania.

Many Christians are reluctant to believe that God would reveal his truth and purpose in a dream or make miracles happen like in the Old Testament. I did not grow up in a Pentecostal tradition, and neither did

Akiane, but we both believe God is as big as he ever was, that God can still speak in any way he chooses. This seems so obvious to me. When asked why she talks about God so much. Akiane responded, "Because he listens. Nothing comes from nothing. Love cannot come out of nothing. Love is God's light. I just can't help talking about it." And I hope she never stops.

Decades before Akiane was born, a young girl named Marguerite Johnson was experiencing a childhood filled with turmoil and strife. Few could have guessed then that the suffering she experienced as child would lead her on a journey that would one day make her one of the most celebrated and passionate poets of our time.

> "I was a mute from the time I was seven and a half until I was almost 13. I didn't speak. I had a voice, but I refused to use it."
> —Maya Angelou

Marguerite's parents divorced when she was just three years old, so she was sent to live with her brother in Arkansas. This brother gave her the nickname "Maya" when she was fairly young. Maya remembers growing up in the world of racial segregation, where blacks were not permitted to fraternize or socialize publicly with whites. She vividly remembers a time when she and her brother went to see a movie, and they couldn't go in through the main entrance. They had to walk around the side, crawl through a door, and sit on little benches. Maya said she felt bad about this because she took it personally—she knew this unfair treatment was because she was black.

PAIN AND SILENCE

When Maya was seven years old, she went to visit her mother in Chicago, and something terrible happened to her there. She was raped by her mother's boyfriend. Maya was too afraid and ashamed to tell any of the adults she knew, but she went and told her brother, because she couldn't keep it inside any longer. She later learned that some of her relatives had beaten her mother's boyfriend to death. Maya fell silent and refused to speak for five years, because she felt as though she had killed the man by talking. Can you really blame her? I can't even imagine the pain and confusion she would have felt, first being abused and ashamed, and then feeling responsible for a man's death.

Maya began speaking again around the age of 13 and soon realized she had a passion for theater and dance (talk about irony!. After high school she received a scholarship to study dance and drama at San Francisco's Labor School. She went to school there and also became San Francisco's first female cable car conductor. In 1952 she married a man named Tosh Angelos. The couple divorced later, but Maya began using a variation of his last name as her stage name, calling herself Maya Angelou. She starred in several dance productions and musicals before moving to New York, where she became a part of the Harlem Writers Guild. As a member she worked with several other young African American artists associated with the civil rights movement. Her association and belief in this movement stuck with her for the rest of her life.

Angelou moved around the world for years, including time in Egypt and Ghana, and she eventually mastered French, Spanish, Italian, Arabic, and Fanti. It was in Ghana where she got to know controversial civil rights leader Malcolm X, whose famous belief that all whites were "blue eyed devils" was growing more balanced and inclusive. She returned to America in 1964 to help Malcolm X build his new organization, but Malcolm X was assassinated before the group really got started.

Maya Angelou also worked closely with my hero, Martin Luther King Jr. She believes Malcolm X and Dr. King are more similar than people may think. She says both men "wanted the best for their people." King asked Angelou to serve as the coordinator for one branch of his organization, and she agreed. When he was assassinated, she was distraught. Maya's friend, the novelist James Baldwin, encouraged her to write as an outlet for her grief.

Maya Angelou's first book, *I Know Why the Caged Bird Sings*, was released in 1970. The book tells the story of Maya's childhood and has become a highly respected work. She also wrote the first screenplay written by a black woman that was ever filmed—and it was nominated for a Pulitzer Prize. But she is probably most widely known as a poet.

Maya has found great success in a field that many people say is dead—poetry. Personally, I've been dying to write a book of poetry, and I know she'd encourage me to go for it. Maya Angelou believes poets should go to the leaders of our churches and say, "I would like to read some poetry in the next assembly, service, meeting." We should start out at home, and maybe it will go other places from there.

Both Akiane and Maya create art from personal experiences—and in doing so, they give voice to things many of us think and feel. Artists have the ability to paint, write, or sing in ways that not only make the world a more beautiful place but also provide for others words and images that expresses their own deepest thoughts and desires. In our world where technology and innovation are so highly valued, young people who are gifted in the arts sometimes feel like they don't fit in or don't have much to contribute. Many schools don't even have art, music, or theater classes anymore. We applaud students who excel in academics and athletics—and we should. But you have to wonder if artists like Maya, Akiane, and so many others are being appreciated and honored for their unique skills and accomplishments.

I hope these two stories provide encouragement for you if you're an artist. If your passion is art—in whatever form—you should pursue it. Whether you are an aspiring filmmaker, a photographer, a painter like Akiane, or a writer like Maya, ask God how you can be a part of bringing the good, true, and beautiful to the world. Let your creativity be used by God to help others.

LOSE YOUR COOL, DISCOVER YOUR PASSION

Akiane clearly has a very special gift. Do you believe God desires to give good gifts, talents, and abilities to all his children?

Why do you think God might choose to give such a unique gift to someone like Akiane?

What are some gifts God has given you that he might want you to use for him and for others?

Maya drew on her painful past and the struggles she witnessed to write her poetry. What pain and difficulties have you been through that God might want to use for good? (This might not be something you want to share with a group, but it might be good to write it down and work through it with God.) If you've been through something tough, ask God to show you what he'd like to do with it.

Have you ever seen artwork or read a poem that moved you or filled you with wonder? Describe this.

How do you feel when you hear of a struggle like Maya's? Have there been other situations that have made you feel the same way?

THE ARTIST WITHIN

As you've probably gathered by now, I love art. I really admire people who can create something beautiful out of nothing. I also like to explore new ideas for making art more accessible for the average person.

One of my favorite companies is Jedidiah—a group that makes clothing with some of the coolest art you'll ever see. They also use their art, clothing, and Web site to do good and help the poor. One of their artists is named Kelli Murray. She designs many of the shirts for Jedidiah, but also does large murals and other artwork you need to check out. And you can be confident when you buy clothing from Jedidiah that all the products are made slave-free. Check them out at www.jedidiahusa.com.

Another fun place to explore your own inner artist is www.zazzle.com—where you can create your own custom T-shirts, shoes and other products. Why wear the same corporate logo millions of other folks are sporting when you can make something truly original? (If you're not sure what image to use, see the box on this page for an idea.)

Bonus Material

At www.loseyourcoolbook.com, you can get free downloads of artwork that 15-year-old Luke O'Kelley created especially for this book. You'll also find two pieces inspired by the chapter on Keith Green at the end of this book. Check them out!"

A CONVERSATION WITH AMENA BROWN

Amena Brown is a spoken-word artist and poet. I've heard her perform a couple of times—she's a passionate communicator who is helping resurrect the art of the spoken word. Here are some of her thoughts about her craft and passion.

Zach: Is there a process you go through when writing a piece? Where do you find inspiration?

Amena: It all depends on the piece. Most of the time the idea kind of stirs around in my head for a while before it makes it out on the page. Poems are funny things. Every time I concentrate and sit down with the goal of writing a poem, nothing comes out. Then at some other inopportune time—early in the morning or right when I lay down to go to sleep—all the lines will show up! I sometimes feel like poems have a mind of their own.

Sometimes I am asked to write poems about a particular subject or theme. Of course, in these cases, I can't wait for the lines to show up when they'd like to, so I tend to read a lot on the subject or theme and write on the theme as often as I can. Some days I may write two lines, and another day, I may write ten or twelve, but eventually enough lines come together to build a poem. After a few drafts I usually come up with something I feel good about.

Inspiration comes from all kinds of places. I write a lot to music, especially jazz—John Coltrane, in particular. Sometimes just listening to jazz music will bring out some words for me. I am definitely inspired by life, things I experience, hard and tough times to really happy times. I also find myself inspired by history and the past. Sometimes I write about memories that I didn't even know I remembered. Reading is also inspirational to me. Something about reading works that are well written inspires me to write as well.

Zach: Who has impacted you most as an artist?
Amena: I would say my mom and dad both played major roles—my mom because of her love for words and history and my dad because of his love for music. Both of them exposed me to great music and great literature early on in life.

I would also say my art was heavily influenced by Rev. Claudette Copeland. She is the copastor of the church I grew up in. I always called her Pastor C. She was a fiery preacher, and she and her husband, Bishop David Copeland, invited many women speakers to our church. It really inspired me to see those women preach, and even at a young age, I felt like I was called to speak in front of people. At the time I had no idea poetry would be a part of that. I think it helped me to see other women doing what I hoped to do. That let me know that what I dreamed was possible.

Zach: What is passion?
Amena: Passion is an innate drive to achieve, accomplish, or change something. All people have certain things they love to do—things they would stay up late and get up early for. Passion gives you the determination to do that. I also think passion stems from wanting to be a part of something that is bigger than you, something that will matter in the world long after you have left it.

Zach: Who are the most passionate people you know?

Amena: Some of the most passionate people I know are entrepreneurs. I think it takes a lot of passion and drive to conceive and build a business from the ground up, to forge a path and make a way where no way has been made before. Anyone who has to pioneer their way to success is a passionate person to me, because it takes dogged determination to keep going and not give up despite all the obstacles and disappointments that may come your way.

Zach: What is your passion?

Amena: My passion is to help people live their lives to the fullest—whether that means discovering their calling, upgrading their social life, experiencing more of the arts, or knowing God in a more personal way. I want to help people make the most of what they have and where they are.

Zach: When did you realize you had a gift for the art of the spoken word? How did this come about?

Amena: I started writing poetry when I was 12 years old. My mom was an avid reader, and she always exposed my sister and me to museums, bookstores, and greeting cards stores. Because of her, I always had a love for words. I realized I had a gift for performing poetry when I was 17. I performed my first spoken-word piece in front of my classmates and teachers, and I knew in that moment that people couldn't be leaning in to listen to a 17-year-old girl. I knew the reason people listened was because the gift to write and speak came from God.

I believe God gives each of us dreams, gifts, and talents. Not so we can become famous or well known. He gives us dreams, gifts, and talents so people can know him. It's my hope and prayer that people see him in the words I write and say and in the life I live.

Zach: Do you think that art can help people in uncovering their passion? How?

Amena: I think art comes from passion in a lot of cases, and it can be a universal language of sorts. Art can sometimes transcend culture and generation. I think that helping people tap into the simple desire to express, to understand and be understood, which art can do so easily, can help many people discover what they are passionate about.

Sometimes people feel they are not passionate or gifted because they don't do a particular art, but that's not true. The world needs all kinds of passionate people, and I think each of us has a part to play by pursuing the dreams that God puts in our hearts.

Bonus Material

Log on to www.loseyourcoolbook.com to read a piece Amena wrote especially for our generation.

SHANE & MILLARD

||||| INTERNING WITH *WHOM?* ||||||||||||

Over the past few years I've had the opportunity to spend some time with a radical guy named Shane Claiborne. Shane looks like the picture I have in my head of John the Baptist. He's this tall, thin, white guy with dreads, who makes his own clothes because he doesn't want to risk supporting a company that uses slave or child labor. Shane lives in a commune in Philadelphia—but it's not your typical monks-and-nuns commune, and it's definitely not some gated retreat out in the boonies somewhere. This commune is a couple of houses in the middle of a section of north Philadelphia that's long been plagued by poverty.

Shane and his friends chose this neighborhood as the spot where they would live, get involved, and make a difference. The folks who are part of this community share a single car, take turns cooking food, and plant flowers in discarded household appliances. Some people may think it sounds crazy, but what they're about is reducing their carbon footprint, consuming less, and helping their neighbors more—neighbors living on that block in Philly as well as neighbors around the world.

Shane and his friends got an interesting start to their Little Revolution. Shane had heard about this amazing nun named Mother

Teresa and her sacrificial work among the poorest of the poor in India. He thought it would be cool to talk with her and learn from her. So he picked up the phone. I don't know if he *really* expected to speak to her directly, but get this—when he finally got through, the person who answered the phone was actually Mother Teresa! On the call she invited Shane and his friends to come to Calcutta and learn how to serve the poor. So he left the United States and went to India where he interned while finding his larger purpose and passion. Now, that's a crazy idea—interning with Mother Teresa! People think the possibility of apprenticing under Donald Trump is a long shot!

> "May the God who gives endurance and encouragement give you a spirit of unity among yourselves as you follow Christ Jesus."
> —Romans 15:5

Shane and his friends took what they learned in India, moved into one of the poorest neighborhoods in Philadelphia, and founded the Simple Way. And now they spend their days investing in relationships and building community on Potter Street.

But what Shane and the Simple Way community are doing is not really a new idea. Since back in the days of the disciples, people of faith have lived in community to share the burdens and joys of life and to stay accountable. The story I'm about to tell you is of a man who learned this several decades ago.

A FRESH START

Millard Fuller's path to life in community was slightly different from Shane's. Millard went to law school after college and became a self-made millionaire by the age of 29. But as he grew in favor in the business world, his marriage began to suffer. Here was a man who had seemed to have it all together, yet the relationship that should have mattered most was taking second place. He knew something had to change.

It was at this point that Millard and his wife, Linda, decided to do something drastic. They sold all their possessions, and they gave their money to the poor. Okay, I know this sounds really crazy to most of us—and actually kind of scary. But it's worth noting that this is exactly what Jesus told another rich guy he needed to do if he wanted to get his life straightened out (see Mark 10:21). And I think there's something kind of invigorating about the thought of someone who is so at the end of his rope that he would choose to do something like this. People often say they wish they could have a fresh start. Well, this was a fresh start for the Fullers.

From that point on their lives took several interesting turns. After they sold everything, they left for Florida to spend some time together as a family and consider what their next steps would be. On the way back they stopped in Georgia to have lunch with some people in a community called Koinonia (coin-oh-KNEE-uh) Farm. *Koinonia* is a Greek word that means "fellowship" or "community." But the Greek word is never used to describe an inactive fellowship—like a group of people who get together just for the sake of gathering. Rather, *koinonia* means something more like, "the act of being in fellowship or communion." So the name implies a group of people who actively seek out opportunities to participate in relationship together, to work together, and to share together on a deeper level. This description is perfect for this small group of people who lived on that farm in rural Georgia.

UPSETTING THE STATUS QUO

Koinonia Farm was founded in the 1940s—that's back before Mother Teresa started her own religious order—by a man named Clarence Jordan. The farm was located in Americus, Georgia, deep in the South—I mean the deep, *deep* South. The community's premise was simple: Koinonia was a place where blacks and whites worked together, ate together, and studied the Bible together as equals. But to the people of Americus, this in itself was a problem. Blacks and whites living together as equals wasn't just countercultural; it was diametrically opposed to the status quo. You see, this was before the civil rights movement, when schools and other institutions were legally segregated. In fact, if you were a black person living in Americus, you had to pay a "walking around" tax. Basically, if you walked around town and hadn't paid this tax, you were arrested!

The majority of the people in Americus did not believe God had created everyone equal. But Clarence Jordan, an unassuming white man, had a different idea. He believed God is the father of every person, regardless of race. And he also believed people could live together peacefully, without violence. Unfortunately, many people in the surrounding area didn't agree. They thought some of Jordan's behaviors were suspicious—things like paying black and white workers equally and having everyone eat at the same table. It's not that Jordan was trying to force other people in the town to sit with each other or to live together like they were doing at Koinonia. It was the simple fact that this was being done at all that irritated people.

That's the way hatred and bigotry work. Bigoted people, by definition, have no tolerance for someone else thinking or behaving differently. One town spokesperson said the problem with the people at Koinonia was that their behavior challenged "conventional wisdom"—meaning the thinking of the majority.

One event that really upset the people of the town occurred when an Indian student was visiting the farm, and some people from Koinonia decided to take him to church. When the white deacons of the church saw him, they were outraged because he was not "one of them." They got together and had a meeting. By the next Sunday the church had passed a policy that said *no one* from Koinonia Farm was allowed in the church.

MORE TROUBLE

This was only the beginning of their problems. When the Supreme Court made its decision in the famous *Brown v. Board of Education* case on May 17, 1954, it greatly agitated many whites in Americus. The *Brown* case was about the integration of U.S. public schools, something widely opposed by many in the South. When integration finally became the law, racists in Americus took action to oppose this radical change in culture.

Over the next few years, racists often targeted Koinonia. Stores owned by Koinonia were bombed or burned by the KKK, which was, and still is, alive and active. The town held a boycott of products produced on the farm. When Koinonia Farm planned an integrated summer camp for children,

There's something kind of invigorating about the thought of someone who is so at the end of his rope that he would choose to do something like this. People often say they wish they could have a fresh start. Well, this was a fresh start for the Fullers.

the county government filed a legal injunction to prevent the camp, saying the buildings were hazardous. But when the health inspector came, he found nothing wrong.

When Clarence Jordan went to Atlanta to work with people who were leading the way in racially integrating schools, this further angered many in the town. During one children's camp, men drove through the area and shot over the kids' heads. One night, when three children were reading bedtime stories, bullets ripped through the wall just inches from their heads. Crosses were burned outside people's homes numerous times. The violence and harassment got so bad that they had to evacuate large numbers of people to another location. Jordan sent a letter to President Eisenhower asking for help, but received a curt reply from the Attorney General that basically said the government could intervene only if a law were being broken.

At the time the local press was painting Koinonia as evil—calling them Communists, and claiming that Koinonia was the source of the violence. But over the years others were drawn to Koinonia, seeing it as a source of hope. During the 1960s a lot of people from the hippie movement who were tired of the "system" flooded Koinonia, encouraged by the fellowship they found there. And this is when the Fullers become part of the Koinonia story. Returning from their trip to Florida after selling all their stuff, Millard and Linda were welcomed by Koinonia; they sat on wooden apple crates and ate dinner there with their new friends. Impressed by the community and warmth they felt at Koinonia, the Fullers decided to move there in 1968.

Much of the information about Millard Fuller, Clarence Jordan, and Koinonia Farm was drawn from the award winning PBS-documentary, *Briars in the Cotton Patch*. You can order the film at www.koinoniapartners.org.

Through all of this the members of Koinonia were constantly trying to figure out how to help in the local community. Millard and Clarence noticed a greet need for affordable housing in the area, so they founded the Koinonia "Fund for Humanity" to help meet this need. This was the beginning of Habitat for Humanity, a nonprofit organization that builds homes for people all over the world, impacting the lives of not only the working poor, but also those who have helped build the houses.

Despite their many successes and all they were doing for the local people, white supremacists in the town still discriminated against Koinonia. Yet the fellowships at Habitat and Koinonia were undaunted—they still powered through and continued loving people no matter what.

DEATH OF A LEADER BUT THE DREAM LIVES ON

In October of 1969 Clarence Jordan died suddenly while writing a sermon. He was buried in his overalls. No people of prominence attended the funeral, but the poor people in the town all came. He transformed thousands of lives—including the lives of people who were born after his death. Think of this: If it weren't for Clarence Jordan, Koinonia wouldn't have existed. If Koinonia didn't exist, the Fullers wouldn't have had any reason to stop in Americus. If Fuller had never come to Koinonia, Habitat for Humanity might never have been created.

Today Habitat for Humanity spans the globe. Koinonia Farm continues today, too, and their ministry includes distributing fair-trade coffee and other products. Americus, Georgia, is the site of the headquarters not only for Habitat and Koinonia, but also for the home of a newer ministry the Fullers launched after leaving Habitat. Today, the Fuller Center for Housing is helping to provide homes for the working poor around the world, working all over the United States and in 15 other countries.

What probably amazes me most about the Fullers is their choice to give away all their possessions, to start over by investing in people rather than things. I was recently talking with my friend Jack Mooring about the devastating financial losses our country has been going through while I have been writing this book. Some people think this is the time to hoard our assets and find ways to protect ourselves financially. Jack was saying that in God's economy, things are totally different. It's at times like these that we should be asking, "What do I have that might help someone else? How can I give away what I have for the use of the kingdom, rather than thinking I don't have enough to get by?"

We should realize that our loving Father owns everything in the world. And since he takes care of the sparrows, how much more will he take care of us? If our passion is to use what we have to show God's love to all people, including those in greatest need, how does that change the way we live? The stories of people like Shane Claiborne and Millard Fuller can help put a lot of our financial choices into perspective.

I have a friend named Stayko (STY-coe), who achieved great success by our world's standards while he was still a very young man. Now in his 20s and in a situation where he could afford just about anything he wanted, Stayko chooses to live in a basement apartment with a group of other guys. He does this purposefully. He wants community; he wants accountability with others; he wants to invest in people; and he feels the best way to journey through life is to do so alongside others, in community, maximizing what you have and sharing what you can. That is true *koinonia*.

Courtesy of Fuller Center for Housing

Author's note: As I was finishing this manuscript, Millard Fuller died at the age of 74. He is now in heaven, in fellowship with his friend, Clarence Jordan, as well as their brother and friend, Jesus. As Millard requested, he was buried in a simple pine casket under the towering pecan trees at Koinonia Farms.

LOSE YOUR COOL, DISCOVER YOUR PASSION

Read Matthew 19:16-28. How is this like Millard Fuller's story? What other choices could Millard have made?

What do you think Matthew 19 requires of us? How might this impact your life and your view of your possessions, influence, and commitment to God? Do you think God requires everyone to give up everything to follow him?

What do you think Shane, Millard, and Clarence are or were passionate about? What kind of courage did it take each of them to pursue the passion he had?

When you think about giving up your possessions, how does this make you feel?

Read Leviticus 19:10 and Leviticus 23:22. How might this principle of purposefully planning to provide for the poor be applied today in different situations?

Why do you think these passages end with "I am the Lord your God"?

WELCOME HOME

Carlos and Santos Rodriguez are a newly married couple with a baby daughter, Gloria Pamela. They live in El Salvador, in a very small tin house built on Carlos' grandmother's land. The young family's tin house leaks and has no windows. The conditions are not healthy for bringing up their baby. They share a very dirty latrine with the rest of the family.

Carlos and Santos are madly in love and believe in working toward a brighter future for their newborn baby. They both dropped out of high school temporarily as young teenagers to help their own families. But now, Carlos is finishing high school in Escuela Santa Clara and also works as a librarian in the school. On weekends he works as a waiter at a beach resort to make extra money.

Santos used to work in the town of El Rosario at a company called Lubricentro, where she was in charge of keeping the inventory at the warehouse. El Rosario is far from Santa Clara, so she had to quit the job after she got pregnant. Currently, she's at home taking care of baby Gloria Pamela. She is also in the process of finishing high school on weekends. In a few months she wants to find a job, and her mother has offered to care for the baby during the day.

This couple is a great example of people who live in great poverty, yet are hardworking and determined to succeed in life no matter what sacrifices they have to make. They are loved and respected by their neighbors and family. Carlos is performing the required sweat equity for the family's Fuller Center house, and Santos volunteers with the Fuller Center. The passion of Millard Fuller, birthed out of a desperate decision to sell it all, continues to benefit people around the world.

(Used by permission of the Fuller Center for Housing, www.fullercenter.org.)

||||| **IN THE BEGINNING** ||||||||||||

When Keith Green was in his early 20s, like many people in that stage of life, he was trying to figure out who he was. And he wasn't just questioning what he was going to do for a profession; he wanted to know the reason for everything in the universe. He was on a search for truth, a search that led him down some dark and treacherous roads before he finally found the answer he was looking for.

Keith's life started with great promise and big hopes. He was born in the early 1950s in New York. His family noticed his musical talent when he began playing ukulele at just three years old, and he soon progressed to guitar and then piano, learning them all by the age of eight. As a child he acted in a few stage productions and also starred in several commercials and a TV pilot. By the time he was eleven, he'd already written 40 songs. That's when he signed a five-year contract with a major recording company called Decca Records.

Decca had big plans for Keith, hoping to make him a preteen "pop idol." This was the beginning of the era when teenage pop stars like Donny Osmond, David Cassidy, and Michael Jackson were topping the charts. (I bet you've heard of Michael Jackson, but you can ask your parents if you don't recognize the others—I'm sure they can help you out.) Keith's first song as a professional recording artist,

"The Way I Used to Be," was released in May 1965. But Keith never achieved the stardom of these other teen talents, and he was soon out of the spotlight and forgotten by the public. Although he continued to write and play music with his friends, Decca didn't renew his contract after the initial five years were up.

"JESUS FREAKS"

Keith came from a Jewish background, yet he often read the New Testament as a kid, and his parents eventually converted to Christian Science. But he grew disillusioned with established religion and joined the movement of young people searching for enlightenment.

> "To obey is better than sacrifice. I want more than Sundays and Wednesday nights."
> —Keith Green, "To Obey Is Better Than Sacrifice"

He was a hippie—with all of the baggage that comes with the title. Many people think of the 1960s as this romantic time where everyone loved everyone and peace reigned on earth, a time when girls wore flowers in their hair and danced in meadows. But that was not what the experience was for Keith and many others who participated in that culture. Hungering for spiritual truth, Keith got involved with drugs, and soon became dependent on LSD. He believed in some sort of god, but he wasn't sure who or what it was and if it was even accessible.

He moved to Seattle to try to start a "spiritual band with a spiritual message," although he seemed unsure what type of spirituality that was. He knew he didn't agree with the Christians, whom he called "Jesus Freaks." A journal entry he made concerning an encounter with these characters at the time makes it clear that he'd begun to think of God as a loving Father, and Jesus as his brother. He said, "They tried to trip on me about believing the whole Bible, word for word, even the part that says God kills my brother and I just don't believe that. Not my wonderful Father!" In the same journal entry, he also said, "I'm still trusting my bro Jesus Christ and Father God, who are one together, and one with me, and we're one with everyone. But it's easier to say that the universe and everything in it is one!"

THE SEARCH

As Keith's belief system became more and more of a mix between Universalism, astrology, mysticism, and Christianity, he also diversified his drug intake. He was now using marijuana, mescaline, and acid regularly. Ultimately this cocktail of drugs and religion never satisfied him. He continued searching, searching, searching. He soon married his live-in girlfriend, Melody, and they continued their search together.

Melody has said that Keith's religious views became more focused around this time. Through all of his searching, he discovered that most of the major religions he had explored gave credibility to Jesus. Jews acknowledge Jesus was a rabbi and a good teacher; Muslims believe he was a great prophet; and Buddhists believe his teaching was honorable. Keith decided that if everyone thought Jesus was "all right" (as the song goes), maybe he should check him out further. Keith and Melody began to study Jesus' words and slowly weaned themselves from drugs as they continued their spiritual journey. Eventually Keith concluded that, since Jesus is so highly respected by all these other religions, then what Jesus said about himself—that he was "the Way"—was probably true.

Keith and Melody's search eventually led them to a small church named Vineyard Christian Fellowship in Beverly Hills. There they found acceptance and many of the answers to their questions and their hearts' desire. They made decisions to turn the control of their lives over to Jesus. Like most things Keith did, he pursued his new Christian faith wholeheartedly—he was completely sold out for Jesus Christ. He told everyone he met about his newfound love.

LAST DAYS

Shortly after their conversions Keith and Melody Green began helping other people in Los Angeles. They purchased the house next to their own, and rented five additional houses in the same neighborhood to provide care for prostitutes, drug addicts, and the homeless. This activity was looked down upon by their neighbors. This reminds me of the story in Matthew 9:10-11:

> "Keith was intense about everything."
> —Melody Green

While Jesus was having dinner at Matthew's house, many tax collectors and "sinners" came and ate with him and his disciples. When the Pharisees saw this, they asked his disciples, "Why does your teacher eat with tax collectors and 'sinners'?"

In 1977 Keith and Melody named their neighborhood outreach effort Last Days Ministries. Every night after dinner Keith would get his guitar out and lead the people who'd gathered there in collective, impassioned worship.

Seeking to combine his love of music, his love for people, and his commitment to Jesus, Keith signed a contract with the Christian music label, Sparrow Records. The music on his first album, *For Him Who Has Ears to Hear*, and its follow-up, *No Compromise*, was ground breaking. Not only were the lyrics hard-hitting and penetrating, the music itself was at the forefront of the new Contemporary Christian Music movement. Pull-no-punches lyrics, like "Jesus rose from the grave, and you can't even get out of bed" ("Sleeping in the Light") and "To obey is better than sacrifice, he doesn't need your money, he wants your life..." ("To Obey Is Better Than Sacrifice"), cut to the heart of some listeners and greatly offended others.

Thankfully Keith didn't really care if he offended people. But he *did* care about the people themselves, and this was obvious to those closest to him. If he told the truth and people were offended by it, well, that couldn't be his concern—there was too much at stake.

Keith was a maverick before anyone knew about John McCain or Sarah Palin. He wrote into his contract with Sparrow that for every one of his cassettes purchased at a Christian bookstore (let's share a moment of silence for the cassette), the buyer would get a second cassette free to give to a friend. He just wanted as many people as possible to hear the good news about Jesus.

After touring for a while, selling records, and gaining more popularity, Keith made a radical decision. In 1979 he walked into the office of the president of Sparrow Records and said, "I blew it. God just told me to start my own label and give my records away. I'm really sorry." [http://www.furious.com/perfect/keithgreen.html] Amazingly the record company let him out of his contract. From that point on Keith only accepted donations for his records. He was determined that nothing should stand between people and the truth—and also painfully aware of the danger of allowing his music ministry to become more about business than about spreading the gospel.

Keith and Melody mortgaged their house so they could produce and sell records. His next album, *So You Wanna Go Back to Egypt*, featured Bob Dylan playing harmonica on both the title track and another song, "Pledge My Head to Heaven." Keith was undoubtedly the most prominent and influential voice in the Christian music world at the time, yet he never changed. He maintained the same desperate, breathless vocal delivery; he still called for open confession of sin;

and, most radical of all, he still believed Jesus was the way to God, the embodiment of truth, and our guiding light.

LIVING IT OUT

If you made a "passion scale" with levels from one to ten, Keith Green would be off the charts. Keith Green took God at his word, and preached the gospel—even when it was unpopular with the über-religious, lukewarm Christians around him. Keith would often write about how God doesn't need our cash and doesn't want just our Sunday mornings and Wednesday nights, he wants our entire lives. In "How Can They Live without Jesus," Keith sings this about his Lord and Savior:

> ...He's not just a religion with steeples and bells,
> Or a salesman who will sell you the things you just want to hear.
> For his love was such that he suffered so much,
> To call some of us just to follow, follow.
> So many laughing at Jesus,
> While the funniest thing that he's done,
> Is love this whole stubborn rebellious world,
> While their hate for him just goes on.
> And love just like that will bring him back,
> For the few he can call his friends.
> The ones he's found true who've made it through,
> Enduring until the end.

Keith Green believed Jesus is not just loving, but the very embodiment of love. To Keith, the God of the Bible is a God of justice, a God who cares about the poor, the needy, and the unsaved. Keith told people the truth with great passion and left the choice up to them.

On July 28, 1982, Keith and two of his children died tragically in a plane crash in Texas. It was a shock to his generation—people felt they'd lost a voice and a shepherd.

Everyone who knew Keith and his music mourned the loss of this amazing man. My mom remembers exactly where she was and what she was doing when she learned of Keith's death. As a young Christian in a non-Christian family, my mom found great spiritual encouragement in his music.

Keith Green impacted countless lives and continues to do so. I was recently at EMI Records—the parent company of Sparrow Records—and a friend there told me that even today, when she asks Christian artists about their influences, many of them still cite Keith Green as a musical mentor.

"JUST A CHRISTIAN"

After reading about Keith Green, you might think to yourself: "Wow, he sounds so amazing. I could probably never be like him. How could anyone follow Jesus so recklessly?" But I had a chance to talk with Melody Green a little while ago (a huge honor, by the way), and she dispelled the idea that Keith was any kind of Christian superhero. "He was really a normal person," she said, "and he loved people—he really recharged being with people."

Melody does say that Keith had more energy than anyone else she's ever known. Maybe God gave him that energy and strength knowing Keith's time would be short. I don't know. Melody recalls: "Keith was intense about everything. He was intense about his favorite flavor of ice cream, about how he made a burger—but especially about Jesus." That intensity comes through loud and clear when you hear his music, read his lyrics, or watch his live concerts. The man was an intense worshipper. An intense lover of people and God.

When I asked Melody what she wanted Keith to be remembered for, she said, "I'd want him to be remembered for what he wanted to be remembered for: Keith Green, 'just a Christian.'" And Keith was just a Christian—but he was on fire for God. He was a radical. And he was part of a movement that shifted a generation and that continues to this day. As Melody told me, "I still get letters all the time from people who have listened to his music, who weren't even alive when he died, saying that their lives have been changed."

Personally, I consider Keith to be a prophet. Now, there are two kinds of prophets (besides the false ones): There are prophets who predict future events; and then there are prophets who speak the truth. Keith Green spoke the truth. He reminds me of John the Baptist, but instead of being a voice crying out in the wilderness as John was, Keith was a voice crying out in our cities and at our music festivals. And just as John the Baptist prepared people for the first coming of Christ, Keith was preparing the way for the second coming, telling people, "I really only just want to see you there."

LOSE YOUR COOL, DISCOVER YOUR PASSION

Read Philippians 3:13 and Matthew 4:18-21. Keith Green had to make some significant changes in his life once he decided to really follow Jesus. What were some of those changes and some of the things he needed to turn his back on? How do you see Keith's life reflected in these verses?

Have you ever taken the step of leaving behind the life you're living and moving into a life committed to following Jesus? If so, explain what that was like—what did that decision mean for you and the "old" life you were living? If you haven't made that decision yet and are curious about what it would look like to do so, there's a special section called "Wondering about Jesus?" at the back of this book that might help you. Check it out.

If you've been following Jesus for a while, are there things that are standing in the way of your deepening your relationship with him? Is anything keeping you from discovering a passion he may want to ignite in you? Maybe there are relationships, habits, interests, entertainment, or addictions you need to give over to God. Take a minute to pray and ask God what might be getting in the way of your following him wholeheartedly. What do you need to let go of?

How can the things you listed above (or the things in Keith's old life) prevent you from discovering and pursuing a passion that may change you and change the world?

What are some things you can do this week to clear away some of the noise in your life so you have space not only to pray but also to listen to God?

In my family we play a game together when we're on a road trip—or when we have new friends with us. The game's called "What's Your Favorite?" One person gets to select the category (like cold cereal, place to spend a holiday, or flavor of ice cream) and then each person gets to state his or her favorite.

Nobody likes to be around people who are always talking about what they can't stand and how much they hate it. People are drawn to others who find enjoyment in the big and small things in life and are willing to talk about the thing they enjoy. Many of us are so busy that we find it hard to make time for things we most appreciate about life. We may not be able to take three hours each day to pursue every hobby we might enjoy or every activity we'd like to do, but we can pay attention and really enjoy those moments we have with the people we love or the things we enjoy doing.

Right now, make a list of 22 things that bring you joy. Don't take a lot of time, maybe 60 seconds total, and be specific. This exercise will help you appreciate the little things—and maybe some big things—that bring you joy. I want to encourage you to try to find opportunities to purposefully enjoy these things. Like for me, when it rains, I try to take a few minutes to notice and really appreciate it, to listen to the raindrops hit the metal roof over our porch and see how it changes the way things look around me—the intensity of the green leaves, the deepening of the brown soil. Or, if I'm eating a new kind of ethnic food, rather than just gobbling it down, I try to savor it, thinking about what makes it different from something I've had before. Try to do the same with your favorite things—then share them with others. It might be by taking them along to indulge in a food you really enjoy—or it might just be by saying, "Isn't it incredible how thinking about a warm chocolate chip cookie can make you salivate?"

To get you thinking about your list, here's my own list from the day I was writing this chapter:

1. The movie *Elf* ("I like smiling, smiling's my favorite!")
2. Music
3. Sushi
4. Rainy days
5. Getting letters in the mail
6. Falling leaves
7. Being with friends
8. Eating with my family
9. Ethnic foods
10. Funny personal-experience stories
11. Poetry (Langston Hughes, Akiane Kramarik, Blair Wingo, Emily Dickinson, Amena Brown)
12. Sweets, like warm chocolate-chip cookies, mint chocolate chip ice cream, and dark chocolate
13. Books (especially on rainy days with falling leaves while eating sushi and listening to good music)
14. Thought-provoking song lyrics (Jon Foreman is the best)
15. Well-brewed herbal tea
16. The scent and taste of mint
17. Sunglasses
18. Slippers in the winter
19. Disney-Pixar movies
20. Taking pictures
21. Discovering unique coffee shops with friends I don't get to see often
22. The aisle seat in the exit row

Log on to www.loseyourcoolbook.com to watch a clip of a documentary about Keith Green's life.

WARNING

When I was doing research for this book, I asked lots of people to tell me about the most passionate people they'd ever known or heard about. Nearly every single person started out by talking about incredible people who have accomplished good things. But almost without fail, they would also mention certain people who have become notorious for the evil they have done and the passion with which they seemed to pursue it.

We may look at people whose passion has driven them to do great things and say, "Well, I could never be like them." It's tempting to assume that people like Mother Teresa or Martin Luther King Jr. had something truly exceptional about them—something we don't have—that makes the kinds of accomplishments they were able to achieve impossible for us. As I've said earlier, I believe that's a lie that causes us to minimize what we are capable of doing.

But I hear people say similar things in relation to their own destructive or sinful behavior. People will say things like, "I may lie, but I'm not a murderer." They dismiss their own sin by comparing themselves with others and boasting, "at least I'm not as bad as so-and-so." And that kind of thinking grows exponentially when we start talking about people whose evil actions have made them notorious—people known around the world for the way their own passions have driven them to hatred and deplorable actions. But as we seek to learn what we can from the lives of people with a passion for good, I think it's important that we also consider what we need to learn from those whose passions have driven them to evil.

The world in which we live is full of pain and suffering. You don't have to look far to see evil personified. In my lifetime there has been a massive genocide in Rwanda, a couple of teenage guys killed people and struck terror on the campus of Columbine High School, Joseph Kony has enslaved tens of thousands of children in his Lord's Resistance Army in Uganda, and terrorists flew planes into the World Trade Center in New York, destroying the lives of thousands.

You've probably heard the old saying, "If we don't learn from history, we're doomed to repeat it." I have talked to people who say that when they learned about the genocide in Rwanda they thought, "How could this have gone on with the whole world watching?" And now, just a few short years after that massive ethnic killing, we're looking at some of the same things happening again in the Sudan. What is it that motivates people to do such horrific things, and what do we need to do to ensure that our own passions move us toward goodness, truth, and beauty? Let's look at a couple examples and see what we can learn and how we can help foster a passion for justice.

A PATTERN OF FORCE AND FEAR

Adolf Hitler's name is synonymous with evil. Just mentioning him probably stirs up those "I'm not like him" feelings in you. But it's worth remembering that, at some point, he was a little boy—born into a family who probably had hopes and dreams for him. As a child he wanted to be an artist. Isn't it hard to imagine a man like Adolf Hitler as a little boy, playing innocently? Or to think of him as a young man with a desire to be known and loved, who wants to create art for the enjoyment of others?

Fast forward a few years, and you begin to see that young artist becoming the Adolf Hitler so many of us know and hate. As he began getting involved in politics, he was known for his impassioned speeches and strong leadership. No one really knows, though, how he really developed his dark, disturbed philosophies of government. Some speculate he was trying to repay someone or atone for something. Whatever the source of his views, Hitler was bent on climbing to the top. He was passionate about leading Germany. As he slowly rose to the top of the Nazi party, he started exerting more control over different parts of his homeland. His use of force and fear to control people would quickly become a pattern for Hitler as time went on.

Another signature of Hitler's was deception. He once said, "Make the lie big, make it simple, keep saying it, and eventually they will

Speaking Out

The word *genocide* refers to actions intended to destroy a group of people because of their nationality, ethnical or racial background, or religious beliefs. Genocide is often fueled by a passionate hatred of others. Whether it's the Holocaust, the Rwandan genocide, or the crisis in the Sudan, too many people have stood by silently (and continue to be silent) in the face of these evils. But a brave few have spoken up.

We need to lift our voices on behalf of others who are weak, vulnerable, and victimized by those who are more powerful. To get involved with efforts in the Sudan, check out:

www.savedarfur.org

www.makewaypartners.org

To be come an advocate for child soldiers in Uganda and the Congo, go to:

www.invisiblechildren.com

www.fallingwhistles.com

believe it." Unless you've been living under a rock your whole life, you must know about Hitler's hatred of Jewish people. Not only did he hold flaming anti-Semitic views, but he hated anyone who helped the Jews or had anything to do with them. Hitler had a plan to put action behind his hatred. In one of the most bizarre moves in history, he declared that anyone who was not blond-haired and blue-eyed ought to be "sterilized."

Hitler began a systematic extermination of all people who weren't like him. The Nazis brutally murdered millions of people in death camps—including Jews and their supporters, political opponents, and others viewed as potential troublemakers. Many were annihilated in gas chambers or in human ovens, others died on dissection tables, and others simply passed away due to starvation and disease. All because of one man's passionate hatred and his ability to convince others to follow him.

PASSIONATE ABOUT POWER

As I'm writing this book, teens from around the world are getting ready to gather in a massive display of support for children forced to serve as soldiers in Uganda. You've probably heard of Invisible Children—the organization working to bring awareness to the plight of these children. The Lord's Resistance Army (LRA), headed by Joseph Kony, has abducted tens of thousands of children in Uganda, Africa, and systematically abused, brainwashed, and indoctrinated them, forcing them to serve as soldiers in his revolution. Kony says he's driven by a message he received from God, and he relentlessly pursues and kills people who don't agree with him.

Children who have escaped or been rescued tell the most gruesome and horrific stories of evils they have suffered at Kony's command. Many children have been forced to kill their own family members. Girls are taken as sex slaves. The oppression and torture continues as Kony's people raid villages, schools, and homes during the night, kidnapping children to populate his army. Children throughout Uganda—and now the Democratic Republic of Congo and the Sudan where Kony has spread his terror—live in constant fear. In an effort to avoid being abducted by Kony's army, many children walk miles each night to a village where they can sleep together in relative safety. Then they walk back to their homes each morning, only to do the same again at nightfall. Children who manage to make it out of the LRA must then struggle to rebuild their lives in a part of the world suffering under the weight of desperate poverty and ravaged by conflict.

When a child is abducted in the United States, there are "Amber Alerts," letting local people know a child is in danger. The faces and stories of these children appear on the back of milk cartons and in mailings, in an effort to find and help them. Yet there is little outcry for the many faceless child soldiers held by Kony.

> "The mouth of the righteous is a fountain of life, but violence overwhelms the mouth of the wicked. Hatred stirs up dissension, but love covers over all wrongs."
> —Proverbs 10:11-12

OUT OF CONTROL

I was listening to the news this morning while driving, and I heard that it was the 10-year anniversary of the Columbine massacre. I was seven when that happened, living in Colorado about an hour from the high school where two teenage guys went in and began shooting classmates and teachers before ending their own lives. These guys weren't some unknown, secret sect of high schoolers, nor were they tyrannical leaders who'd been building a following of people to help create a kingdom. They were just a couple of high-school kids, living in a suburb, who became consumed by the idea that they wanted to be famous—and decided the way to achieve that fame was to bomb their high school. Ultimately, they altered that plan, took firearms to school, killed 14 students and one teacher, and left 20 others injured and a whole nation shaken and searching for answers as to how this could have happened.

> "He alone who owns the youth, gains the future."
> —Adolf Hitler

Experts are still trying to make sense of what went on that day. What drove these young men to such acts of violence? There's been lots of speculation: Maybe they were mentally unstable. Maybe they'd been impacted by exposure to violence. Maybe their social status at school had driven them toward lives filled with hatred.

I'm no expert, but what I do know is that their lives were out of control. They obviously were believing a lie. And if there were people in their lives who could have helped them—people who tried to speak the truth to them and show them the path toward God and toward peace—these young men weren't allowing those individuals to have any impact on their lives. Their passion for control and fame led them to violently snuff out the lives of others.

ON OUR WATCH

We might look at Hitler's story or the Rwandan genocide and be outraged that our grandparents and parents could have allowed these horrors to take place. But we need to stand up and take responsibility for what's happening today—both in our individual lives and in the world. What's happening in Africa with child soldiers is occurring on our watch. And it's happening because of one man's passion for power and his ability to recruit others to follow him. People who knew Kony when he was a child say he was a likeable guy, a good athlete with a good sense of humor. He didn't start out as a hideous monster. Yes, he had a sinful nature just as we all do—but at some point he began feeding that nature, surrounding himself with distorted thinking and people who would support him.

I know the stories of Hitler, Kony, and the Columbine students seem extreme. These were people who were bent on evil and consumed by hatred. But how did they get that way? How does a little boy who dreams of becoming an artist develop a passion for destroying life? How does a friendly kid with great potential grow up to abduct, torture, and kill thousands? What makes two teenaged friends decide to play God with other people's lives?

It's clear that it doesn't happen overnight. Seeds of bitterness and anger, if they are nurtured, grow into contempt and hatred. And if that hatred continues to grow unchecked, it will reproduce in the hearts of others. It starts in the secret places, the dark corners, and no one knows about it but us and God. But if we let it stew and brew, it starts to take over every area of our lives. Sometimes, hatred can become so big that we forget where it even started. Jesus said that if you hate someone, you have murdered that person in your heart. Hatred can steal your life if you let it. We need to nip hatred in the bud. Kill it at the source.

I've had the privilege of meeting many other teens from all around the world. And I've noticed that we sometimes feel we have a right to harbor an offense. Someone has wronged us in some way, and we hang onto it. We sometimes even wear it as a badge of honor. But I've seen how the protection of that offense, our owning and embracing it, can rob us of the good things God has for us. It can choke our energy. It can keep us from discovering the passion for good that God has given each of us. When we're holding so tightly to the wrong that's been done to us and the hurt we feel, it's hard to embrace God's plan for us.

If you've been hurt by someone or by your circumstances, please find a trusted adult you can talk with about your situation. Ask them to help you as you release your pain and anger to God and seek to forgive the offender. Maybe you've been the one doing the offending—your words or actions have wounded someone else. It's time to make that right.

It's easy to say we're not evil the way Hitler was—we haven't killed anyone or committed other such atrocities. But his story has something to teach us about our own sinful nature and the potential sin has to destroy us if we feed it and allow it to grow rather than feeding our spirits. It is time for introspection. It's time to lose your cool and get honest with God.

Finding Help

In this chapter I've talked about people who have held on to bitterness or anger so that their pain has taken over their lives and caused them to do violence to others. I want to acknowledge that there are many other people—including several of the other people profiled in this book—who have suffered great pain and suffering, yet have been able, with God's help, to let go of that pain, find healing, and live the full life God desires for them. If you have been abused or are suffering under a weight of fear or hatred, I encourage you to get help. Sometimes we need others to help us through difficult times. If you're dealing with depression or feelings of despair or considering harming yourself, please seek out the help of a professional. Call your pastor, talk to your parents, see your counselor at school—but don't wait to get the help you need. You can also find help on the following Web sites:

www.thehopeline.com

www.twloha.com (there's a great list of resources under the "Find Help" button)

LOSE YOUR COOL, DISCOVER YOUR PASSION

Is there an individual or a group of people whom you hate or have other strong negative feelings about? If so, why do you think these feelings are taking root in you?

Do you find yourself nurturing those negative feelings and justifying the way you feel about this individual or group?

How do you think Jesus feels toward the people you struggle with? How does he feel toward you? If you told Jesus why you hate or dislike them, what do you think you would say?

It can be tempting to try to shape other people's views of individuals we don't like. But here's some interesting direction from God's Word.

"Don't spread gossip and rumors. Don't just stand by when your neighbor's life is in danger. I am God. Don't secretly hate your neighbor. If you have something against him, get it out into the open; otherwise you are an accomplice in his guilt. Don't seek revenge or carry a grudge against any of your people. Love your neighbor as yourself. I am God. (Leviticus 19:16-18, The Message)

If you've been spreading rumors, holding a grudge, or trying to tank someone's reputation, take some time now to confess it and ask God how he might want you to repair the damage you've done. Listen to God and journal about what you believe God is asking you to do.

If you reflect on the life of Jesus, do you think there were people Jesus had good reason to hate—people who worked against him, tried to destroy his reputation, or wanted to hurt or kill him? How did Jesus respond to these people?

Our own hatred toward others may not be rooted in the same righteous indignation Jesus might have felt. Our hatred may be rooted more in selfishness or fear. But since Jesus was able to relinquish his right and freedom to hate, he can also help us do the same. If letting go of this is hard for you, tell Jesus why and ask him for help.

Hitler once said, "He alone who owns the youth, gains the future." But Hitler and Kony surrounded themselves himself with people who affirmed their thinking and fueled their efforts. The two teens from Columbine crafted their plan together. So who is "owning" you—who do you allow to influence your life and thinking? Are you giving ownership of your life to the wrong people? Maybe you're letting the media influence your choices, hanging out with the wrong people, or holding on to the wrong thoughts and ideas. If this is the case, what do you need to do about it?

PROTECTING LIFE

While some people were bent on the destruction of life, others were bent on protecting it, even at the cost of their own. Dr. Janusz Korczak was one such protector during World War 2. For many years Janusz wrote children's books that were famous throughout Europe. Even as the Nazis were occupying Poland and carrying out their systematic extermination of the Jews there, Dr. Korczak started an orphanage in a Polish ghetto for Jewish children.

One day Dr. Korczak received notice that the Nazis were coming for the children. He had an opportunity to escape the country himself, but Dr. Korczak refused to abandon the kids he's been caring for. One Holocaust survivor who watched the soldiers escort the children from the orphanage described it in this way:

> The children were to have been taken away alone. He [Dr. Korczak] had the chance to save himself, and it was only with difficulty that he persuaded the Germans to take him too. He had spent long years of his life with children and now, on this last journey he could not leave them alone. He wanted to ease things for them…He told them to wear their best clothes, and so they came out into the yard, two by two nicely dressed and in a happy mood… When I met them in Gesia Street the smiling children were singing in chorus…and Korczak was carrying two of the smallest infants, who were beaming too, and telling them some amusing story. I am sure that even in the gas chamber, as the Zyklon B gas was stifling childish throats and striking terror instead of hope into the orphans' hearts, the Old Doctor must have whispered with one last effort, "It's all right, children, it will be all right." (Władysław Szpilman, *The Pianist*)

YOU

||||| FUELED BY PASSION |||||||||||||

When I'm out speaking, I often talk to other teenagers who are concerned they haven't found their one big passion. They might hear me talk about the passion I have for the campaign to end slavery, or maybe they hear me share the stories of other passionate people—artists, activists, athletes, and others of faith—who've discovered something that fills their lives with hope and meaning. And they feel frustrated they've not found the one thing they want to spend their own lives doing.

Well, this book isn't about backing you into a corner and forcing you to choose only one thing to spend your time on. This book is about helping you find fulfillment and purpose by using your skills, strengths, and interests. When you tap into the passions of God and begin to explore the unique way he created you and what he might want you to do with that uniqueness, your life will have more meaning. You'll know you're not just passing time or killing time or even spending time, but *investing* time. It's also important to remember that your passions can change and grow. The things you're passionate about today—the things in which you invest your time, energy, and resources now—can change as you have new experiences and discover new things about yourself and the world. So don't worry if you haven't found a single passion that defines what you are all about.

As you are in the middle of finding, working through, and being fueled by your passion, it's important to remember one thing: Discovering your passion is not about making God love you more. Nothing any of us can do will make God love us more or less. God already loves you more than anything else in the whole world. Your passion, and the actions that spring from them, should not be efforts to win God's favor. Instead, they should be an outpouring of your relationship with him. Knowing that God has given you all you have, you give what you have back to God as an offering. As the Bible says, "Whatever you do, do it all for the glory of God" (1 Corinthians 10:31). Whether it's writing, dancing, playing soccer, painting, serving at a soup kitchen, raising money for the homeless, or talking to the new kid—do *everything* as if you are doing it for God. That is a life of passion.

> It's time to lose your "cool" and invest your time and effort into pursuing what God has uniquely equipped you to do and be.
> I really believe there's no such thing as an ordinary person. Every single one of us is created in the image of God, and he has prepared good things for us to do with him.

KEEPING YOUR BALANCE

As is the case with many good things, there's always the potential that our passion for some cause or activity can make us become out of balance. There's a risk that a passion can progress into something dangerous, like an obsession. Maybe you've become aware that there are starving children in other parts of the world—and you want to do something about it. But maybe you have trouble eating because you feel guilty about the children who don't have food. You have trouble sleeping, because you see the starving children in your dreams. You feel guilty that you have enough to eat when others don't, and all you talk about when you're with friends is the starving children. That's not healthy. At that point your healthy passion about this issue has crossed over into an obsession that can damage you and the people around you, and make you ineffective at bringing real, lasting help.

If you are acting or feeling this way, then take a step back and look realistically at the situation. You need to take care of your body, mind, and spirit, and you need people around you who can encourage you and work alongside you in your passion. If you are wringing yourself out and disregarding those around you because your passion has turned to obsession, then you need to ratchet it back a little bit. It's not healthy. I'd encourage you to talk with a wise and trusted adult who can help you find the balance you need and can encourage you to channel your passion in ways that bring health and life for you, others, and your world.

LOSE YOUR COOL

Let's flash back to the very beginning of the book, where we talked about the difference between interests and passions. I think some of us choose our interests because we think those things will fulfill us and make us "cool." If you define yourself by what movies you've seen, what type of iPod you have, or what features are on your cell phone, then you might want to start this book over. It's time to lose your "cool" and invest your time and effort into pursuing what God has uniquely equipped you to do and be.

Sometimes people who know about my speaking and writing ask me if I wish I could just be a normal teen. I usually say it depends what they mean by "normal." If normal means spending the majority of my free time in front of the TV, playing video games, or just laying around—then my answer is "no." I enjoy all these things from time to time, but I've discovered a life that has more joy and more excitement than those things hold.

I hope our generation will redefine "normal." I hope we'll be known as the generation that lived their lives with passion and beauty, that gave themselves up for the poor and oppressed, that loved extravagantly and courageously. I don't always do these things well, but that's how I want to live. And it's how I hope my own life, and my entire generation, will be defined. I hope you'll join me.

You may be someone like Billy Mills or Akiane Kramarik, who's been gifted with an extraordinary ability that can be used to help others, bring goodness and beauty to the world, and offer you a platform to share your faith. Or maybe, like Amy Carmichael, you feel God has ignited a passion in you about some cause or problem—and you want to find a way to make a difference. I really believe there's no such thing as an ordinary person. Every single one of us is created in the image of God, and he has prepared good things for us to do with him. That's an amazing thought.

God loves it when his people explore their passions and discover the joy of allowing him to change us and change the world around us. So let's get started!

Bonus Material

If you've become curious and want to know more about this man, Jesus, whom I've talked about, go to www.loseyourcoolbook.com where I've written a little something to explain what I've learned about him.

LOSE YOUR COOL, DISCOVER YOUR PASSION

What do you think you're good at?

What do other people say you're good at or compliment you on?

Name something you've done for which you received affirmation.

Write about something you've done that brought you joy.

When do you feel closest to God? Are there activities or places that make you sense his presence more?

As you have read through the stories in this book, which ones made you say, "That's so much like me!" or "I wish I could do that?"

What stories in the book stuck with you and came back to mind later? Which topics addressed in the book did you continue to think about after you finished reading?

What's one thing you want to do with your time as a result of reading this book? What new interest would you like to pursue? What current activity would you like to dig into more deeply?

What are some problems that make your heart beat faster? What makes you ask, "Why isn't someone doing something about this?"

Are there issues, themes, or conversations that keep popping up in your life? Are there things you keep reading in Scripture that relate to the same issue? If so, list some of those things here—and ask God if this is his way of getting your attention about something in particular.

Write down a prayer asking God to show you where your God-given talents, abilities, interests, and gifts might be used for his glory.

Take another look at your answers above. Are there ways you can use your talents and interests to address something God has laid on your heart? How might you pursue that further?

Take your ideas and discuss them with a trusted friend—or, if you're reading this book with a small group, discuss your thinking with the people in your group. Ask people what they think about the ideas you've uncovered and see what they say.

ENDNOTES

George

1. www.christianitytoday.com/ch/131christians/evangelists andapologists/whitefield.html
2. www.christianitytoday.com/ch/131christians/evangelists andapologists/whitefield.html
3. www.jesus.org.uk/ja/mag_revivalfires_philadelphia.shtml
4. www.reformationart.com/george-whitefield-1.html

Quixote

1. Adapted from Marshall, James, "The Code of Chivalry," www.astro.umd.edu/~marshall/chivalry.html (accessed October 23, 2008).

Billy & Paul

1. www.fosterclub.com/famous/billy-mills
2. www.loc.gov/loc/lcib/0502/mills.html
3. www.fosterclub.com/famous/billy-mills

Jehanne

1. *Joan of Arc: In Her Own Words*, Walter Trask, trans. (Turtle Point Press, 1996).
2. *Joan of Arc: In Her Own Words*
3. www.breakpoint.org/listingarticle.asp?ID=5970

Bonus Material

Check out this cool artwork by 15-year-old Luke O'Kelley. These pieces were inspired by the story of Keith Green. Go to www.loseyourcoolbook.com to download other free artwork Luke has created. You can save it and make your own gear at www.zazzle.com—or you can print it out, make your own posters and cards, or send it to friends on Facebook. Have fun!

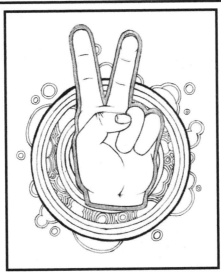

ABOUT THE AUTHOR

Zach Hunter is a sixteen-year-old abolition-ist and activist, and he is inspiring a new generation of activists to put their faith into action and address some of the most seri-ous problems facing the world today. When Zach was twelve he started a campaign called Loose Change to Loosen Chains, help-ing to raise awareness and money to free people from slavery. The author of *Be the Change* and *Generation Change*, and blog-ger for Breakaway, Zach speaks to hundreds of thousands of people each year, encourag-ing them to discover God's great love and make a change in the world. Hunter lives in Atlanta, Georgia, and when he's not busy changing the world, he is your typical teen-age guy.

Many people think teenagers aren't capable of much. But Zach Hunter is proving those people wrong. He's working to end slavery in the world— and he's making changes that affect millions of people. Find out how Zach is making a difference and how you can make changes in the things that you see wrong with our world.

Be the Change
Your Guide to Freeing Slaves and Changing the World
Zach Hunter
Retail $9.99 | 978-0-310-27756-6

Visit www.planetwisdom.com or your local bookstore.

Our world is broken, but you can change that. Zach Hunter is a teenage activist, working to end modern-day slavery and other problems facing the world. He believes your generation can be the one to change our world for the better. Inside you'll read stories of real students changing the world, and find tangible ideas you can use to be the generation of change.

Generation Change
Roll Up Your Sleeves and Change the World

Zach Hunter
Retail $12.99 | 978-0-310-28515-1

Visit www.planetwisdom.com or your local bookstore.

|||||||||||| **NOTES** |||||

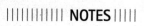

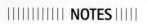
NOTES

 NOTES |||||